*An...*
**Fat...**

The Story of Colonel Ruby G. Bradley
The Most Decorated Woman
in the History of the United States Army

By Nancy Polette

Blessinks
St. Charles, MO
www.blessinks.com

Cover illustration by Paul Dillon

ISBN-10: 0988846527

ISBN-13: 978-0-9888465-2-4

## DEDICATION

To Dr. Evelene Lorton, gracious lady and heroine to thousands of teachers.

Nancy Polette

# Table of Contents

1 The Adventure Begins ........................................... 1

2 The Voyage ........................................................ 17

3 Paradise Found .................................................. 27

4 The Attack ....................................................... 47

5 Escape ............................................................ 69

6 Surrender ........................................................ 89

7 Prisoner ......................................................... 111

8 A Surprise Move ............................................... 133

9 Santo Tomas .................................................... 153

10 Liberation ..................................................... 175

10 On the Front Lines .......................................... 197

APPENDIX ......................................................... 217

CHAPTER NOTES .................................................. 221

ABOUT THE AUTHOR ............................................ 233

Nancy Polette

## FORWARD

The amazing story of Ruby Bradley is an inspiration to all of us. Women have served with distinction since the Revolutionary War but so many of their stories have been lost or never told. I am embarrassed to say; I had not heard of Colonel Bradley until I read this book. Other than my Dad, who served in World War II, I am the only one of seven children to join the military. I did not know any women who had served in the military and I was never exposed to books that highlighted the incredible experiences the military offers to women. The only woman I read about when I was young connected to the military, was Sacajawea, a key member of the Lewis and Clark expedition (The Corps of Discovery).

Colonel Bradley was an adventurer, unafraid of life's challenges. She refused to be left behind in the service of our country. She not only witnessed the history of our nation at war; she made history in her devotion to duty and dedication to every man and woman in uniform. Over 350,000 women served in WWII but only 88 were captured and held as prisoners of war. Colonel Bradley's acts of courage while a POW and while serving in Korea are part of the heritage that has led to the opening of previously denied roles to women in the military.

I joined the military for adventure and to see the world. The Air Force has provided me those opportunities, with the added bonus of serving my country. I have met the most dedicated and interesting people from all backgrounds and parts of our nation. I now have met another hero in uniform, Colonel Ruby Bradley.

Cassie A. Strom, Brig. General, MOANG

ANG Assistant to TJAG

# 1 THE ADVENTURE BEGINS

"YES! YES! YES!" On this late November day in 1939 the excited nurse found it hard not to shout. Even then, her words flew like arrows to a target from her office through the quiet of the hospital ward. Heads popped up from half a dozen beds. The men didn't need to be told what the excitement was all about.

"We'll miss you, Lieutenant," one veteran called out. Other voices joined in, for the trim nurse with dark, curly hair, dancing brown eyes and an easy smile was a favorite with the patients.

"I'll miss you guys, too," Lieutenant Ruby Bradley grinned waving the just-opened orders that would send her to the Philippines for a two-year tour of duty.

Not that Ruby Bradley ever gave less than her best to her patients. Duty hours were forgotten on her ward at Walter Reed Hospital when a patient was critically ill. Watching Ruby holding a hand or wiping a fevered brow in the late night hours was a familiar sight. Still, she could not help looking at her new assignment with the same sense of adventure that led her to join the Army Nurse Corps.

Graduating from Spencer High School in 1926 Ruby knew there were few career choices open to women. One of those choices was teaching so Ruby enrolled at Glenville State Teachers College. Upon graduation she took a job teaching all eight grades in a one-room school near her home in Spencer, West Virginia. Ruby listened to children recite lessons all morning. At noon her pupils opened lunch buckets to reveal cold pancakes or oatmeal from breakfast, a piece of bread spread with lard and sugar, or a piece of cake. Ruby's lunch bag held extra food for those children who did not bring a lunch.

The afternoon brought more lessons until Ruby rang the closing bell. However, her ten-hour day was not over. She swept the room, cleaned the boards and carried in buckets of coal for the pot-bellied stove. She spent her evenings grading papers and writing lesson plans. Despite the long days Ruby was determined to give her best to every child. What pride she felt for a little one who mastered a difficult problem!

While Ruby loved teaching, an inner voice told her that she needed a greater challenge. After four years Ruby made a decision that would change her life forever. A world of adventure was out there somewhere. She had to find it. But what could she do? Jobs were scarce in the Depression years. Twenty-five percent of people were out of work. There were bread lines everywhere to feed the hungry. Fifty dollars a month was a good salary for a single girl. But she needed to grow and to learn and to explore.

"Follow me around for a day," Sally, Ruby's younger sister told her. Sally, an Army nurse loved her job at Walter Reed Hospital.

One visit to her sister's ward at Walter Reed and Ruby discovered a new and exciting world. From the moment she stepped inside the marble-floored halls, heard the swish of starched uniforms as nurses moved quickly through long corridors and listened to the urgent calls from speakers overhead, Ruby made up her mind. This was the career she wanted, not only to be a nurse but to be a top flight surgical nurse assisting at complicated operations. She wasted no time in applying for admission to the Philadelphia General Hospital School of Nursing. It was then she discovered that getting into a nursing program was not easy.

The Depression years took their toll on the nursing profession. Many sick people could not afford to go to the hospital so fewer nurses were needed. Several smaller nursing schools closed and those that remained open were very picky about the new students admitted to their programs.

Ruby was not discouraged. She would do whatever it took to become a nursing student. First came an interview with the Superintendent to determine if she had enough mature intelligence to carry out and obey orders. Next, she obtained a reference from her minister testifying to her good moral character. Last she passed a demanding physical that guaranteed she had sound health and unimpaired faculties. In 1930 only a high school diploma was required for admittance to a nursing school. Ruby's two years of college and experience as a teacher impressed the admissions committee. It was a joyful day when she opened the letter telling her she was accepted.

On July 1 of 1930, Ruby stepped out of a taxi at 3801 Chestnut Street to stand in front of Philadelphia General Hospital. Her eyes quickly took in the main four-story building with smaller wings on each side. This was her dream come true. What adventures waited for her inside these worn brick walls? More than 200 years old, known by many as "Old Blockley," here was a haven for the poor, the sick, the elderly and the insane. Despite its role as a charity hospital Ruby knew that Philadelphia General ranked as one of the greatest municipal hospitals in the world.

It was time to stop daydreaming, Ruby vaulted the steps two at a time, burst through the massive front doors and ran smack into a tall, thin woman in a nurse's uniform almost knocking her down.

"Sorry," Ruby stammered reaching out to steady the woman. "Are you all right?"

The nurse drew herself up to her full height and stared coldly at the embarrassed girl. "Probationers report to room 2220 in the East Wing," she said, turning on her heel. "Don't be late."

"*How did she know I was a probationer?*" Ruby wondered. "*East Wing. Where the heck is the East Wing?*" Ruby entered a long cream colored corridor. The familiar hospital smell of cleaning compound and antiseptics was everywhere. The corridor was empty. *Now what? There!* An overweight man in drab green scrubs was puffing down the corridor pushing an empty gurney.

"Could you direct me to Room 2220 in the East Wing?" Ruby asked.

"End of the corridor, turn right, up the stairs," he called not stopping. *Was everyone in this hospital in a hurry?* She wondered.

Following directions and with minutes to spare Ruby found Room 2220. A host of chattering females told her she was in the right place. Before she could sit down, a freckle-faced girl nudged her. "I'm Martha," she grinned. "Sit with me. Catch your breath. Lucky for you the dragon isn't here yet."

Chatter ceased at once when a hawk-nosed scarecrow of a woman entered the room. Every hair was in place under her starched white cap. Not a speck of dirt dared appear on her crisp white uniform. Ruby moaned. It was the same nurse she almost floored. The one they called "the dragon."

"I am Miss Clayton, Superintendent of Nurses. As first year students you are probationers. Any infraction of the rules posted in your quarters will lead to immediate dismissal. You are never to question authority and must carry out all orders whether given by floor nurses, head nurses, physicians, residents or interns. Punctuality", she said looking directly at Ruby "is a must for both ward duty and classes. Questions should be referred to your instructor or floor supervisor. Miss Barton will show you to your quarters where you will find your uniforms and duty assignments. Welcome to Philadelphia General." With a brisk nod she turned on her heel and left the podium as quickly as she had appeared.

The now silent probationers picked up their bags and followed tiny Miss Barton down the stairs and out the doors of the hospital to nurses' quarters next door. Catcalls and whistles followed the girls as they passed a group of interns smoking on the hospital steps. Entering the building. Ruby and Martha hurried across well-worn floors to the bulletin board where room assignments were posted.

"Get ready to sweat!" Martha groaned as the probationers jotted down the numbers of their third floor rooms. Second year students occupied the lower, cooler floors. Climbing three flights of creaking stairs they found in each room a steel cot, a dresser, a sagging chair and a tiny closet. The walls were bare except for posted regulations. An ancient fan did little except stir the hot July air. Fortunately there were huge windows that could be opened at night. QUIET signs hung on every wall. The night nurses were trying to sleep, not an easy thing to do with the paper-thin walls.

Ruby soon discovered that little time was spent in the nurses' quarters. She fell quickly into a routine. Up at six, breakfast, ward duty from seven until nine. Classes from nine till ten, then back to ward duty from ten until three. More ward work from seven until eleven. However, it was rare that probationers were released at eleven.

Time for study was hard to find. Any free time Ruby slept. She didn't mind the long hours and hard work. Each day was filled with carrying trays, feeding patients who could not feed themselves, cleaning recently vacated rooms, washing countless glasses, pitchers, basins and pans, giving baths, changing beds, stacking linens and making countless runs up and down four floors of steps to get lab results.

What Ruby did mind was biting her tongue no matter what criticism, fair or not, was thrown at her. And, she discovered, many head nurses took delight in finding things to criticize.

"Miss Bradley," Head Nurse Carson called out. It was the end of Ruby's seven to eleven shift.

Answering Nurse Carson's call she found the angry woman in a vacant room. "Did you clean this room today?" she asked.

"Yes, Mam," Ruby answered. Her eyes darted from the freshly made bed, to the gleaming floor and the polished night table. A glance at the closet revealed neatly stacked linens. She saw nothing out of place.

"The pitcher!" Nurse Carson yelled. "The handle is turned the wrong way. A patient could not easily reach it. Before you go off duty you are to wash every water pitcher on this floor and when you return them to the patients' rooms, put the handle in the correct position."

It was midnight when an exhausted Ruby made it to the nurses' quarters. Not bothering to shed her uniform, she fell asleep the minute she hit her bed.

Ruby and Martha, as second year students moved to lower levels in the nurses' quarters. Now the menial tasks gave way to patient care and training for the operating room. But to Ruby's disappointment, student nurses assigned to surgery rarely saw an operation.

Ruby folded dressings and linens, cleaned instruments and put them into the proper sets, patched, powdered and sized rubber gloves, filled suture jars, and assembled surgical packs of gowns, drapes and sponges. Near the end of the second year Ruby proved competent enough to attend simple operations in the amphitheater, working as an extra circulating nurse beside an experienced surgical nurse. Patience paid off. Her last year brought the excitement she craved. As graduation drew near in 1933 she was assisting surgeons as a surgical nurse.

Ruby's knowledge, her good-natured, easy smile, her skills and her gentleness with patients made her a favorite at Philadelphia General. She was asked to stay but the desire for adventure was too strong. One year later, following in her sister Sally's footsteps, on October 16, 1934 she took the Army Officers Oath of Office:

"I, Ruby G. Bradley having been appointed an officer in the Army of the United States, as indicated in the grade of 2nd Lieutenant do solemnly swear (or affirm) that I will support and defend the Constitution of the United States against all enemies, foreign and domestic, that I will bear true faith and allegiance to the same; that I take this obligation freely, without any mental reservation or purpose of evasion; and that I will well and faithfully discharge the duties of the office upon which I am about to enter; SO HELP ME GOD"

Ruby felt a ripple of pride when she put on her Army uniform. She was issued a dark blue blazer and skirt and lighter blue shirt with tie. Her dark blue cape was trimmed with maroon braid. While on duty she wore the same white nurses' uniform she wore at

Philadelphia General. The only difference was the military insignia on the collar.

Ruby's rank as Second Lieutenant was labeled a "Relative Rank." It carried few privileges. The pay was two thirds of the pay of a regular officer. Enlisted men were not required to salute. Because the Army nurses were not considered to be members of the actual army they were not required to undergo basic training. Instead, immediately after joining the army Ruby was assigned to duty at Walter Reed Army Hospital.

It was a blustery day in October 1934 when Ruby reported to Chief Nurse Gertrude Thompson's office at Walter Reed. This time she did not need directions. She had scouted out the hospital days before. Nurse Thompson, who held the rank of Captain, greeted Ruby at the door. "Follow me," she said. Ruby followed her guide down long corridors to the office of the Commander of Walter Reed Hospital, Colonel Keller. Introductions were brisk. "Colonel Keller. Lieutenant Bradley." The senior nurse gave a quick salute did an about face and returned to her duties.

"Busy woman," the Colonel grinned. "Welcome to Walter Reed and our 1225 beds which are nearly always full. We will keep you busy. Captain Thompson will give you your duty assignments," the Colonel told her. "Report back to her office for orientation."

A young lieutenant from the Chief Nurses' office gave Ruby a map of the hospital and what she called "the twenty-five cent tour." Entering the nurse's quarters Ruby saw the familiar bulletin board and the posting of assignments. At 7:00 a.m. she was to observe in operating room four, the first of dozens of operations performed daily at Walter Reed.

Ruby was content. Just as at Philadelphia General, she soon became a favorite with both patients and doctors at Walter Reed. As a skilled surgical nurse her days were full. While not in the operating suites, Ruby spent free time in the wards checking on her post-op patients.

Every surgeon she worked with knew that Ruby would hand him whatever he needed the moment he asked for it. When a surgeon entered the operating room Ruby assisted him with a sterile gown and powdered gloves and handed him a sterile towel. Sterilized instruments where ready for use. Ties for the bleeders, catgut and silkworm sutures for closing wounds, large and small sponges to stop bleeders were at her fingertips to be passed at a moment's request.

Between operations and post-op care of patients Ruby's days were full. Looking after a patient with removal of a gall bladder or appendix became routine. Unfortunately for her the routine surgeries did not prepare either Ruby or the surgeons for the trauma operations they would soon be facing.

ATTENTION! It was Inspection Day. Arriving at the ward before seven, Ruby and the corpsmen straightened beds, folded blankets, cleaned tables, mopped floors and polished anything with a brass handle. The tiniest specks of dust disappeared. The latrines were spotless, linen closets neatly stacked and medications in their proper places.

The ramrod figure of Colonel Keller accompanied by a captain, a sergeant and a corporal stepped into the ward with military precision. Men who were able, saluted. Ruby and the ward attendants stood at attention not moving a muscle. Striding up and down the aisle between the beds, the Colonel's sharp eyes were everywhere. Sheets on every unoccupied bed had neat military corners. Top shelves were dust free. Linens were neatly stacked. He motioned to the Corporal. A tiny speck of rust on a drawer handle must be removed. The corporal pulled out a polishing rag.

"Inspection passed," the Colonel barked doing an about face and leading his group to the next ward.

Ruby let out a sigh of relief. This was her last weekly inspection at Walter Reed. Following a short visit home, in January 1940 she was off to the Philippines. It had been a fourteen-year journey from teacher to student to Army nurse. Now Ruby was about to see her dream for adventure come true. Little did she know that the day was not far off when that dream would become a nightmare.

## 2 THE VOYAGE

It was a blustery January night in 1940 when Ruby and three other army nurses climbed out of the back of an army truck at their Port of Embarkation. Needles of sleet stung their faces. A chilling wind whipped their capes across their shoulders. All four women jumped aside as unseen hands pitched their gear from the back of the truck onto the icy pavement below. Minutes later, with a sputter and backfire the empty truck took off leaving behind the smell of exhaust fumes.

The lonely moan of a ship's horn cut through the dark night. It was impossible for them to get a good look at the ship. Ruby wondered if it was the USS

Hendersen, recently in the news for transporting troops from the States to the Philippines. All the shivering nurses could see was a huge bulky shape... a big, black monster with gleaming porthole eyes. Because of the outbreak of war in Europe, the East Coast blackout was soon to come but had not yet begun. Struggling under the weight of their gear the women followed a line of soldiers through a gaping hole in the side of the towering ship. It made Ruby think of herding cattle.

"Get your rear in gear, kid," a sergeant called to a young Corporal struggling under the weight of a huge duffel bag, a bed roll, a rifle and a steel helmet. Ruby couldn't make out his face. It was lost under all the gear. But she was positive she saw a small shape moving under the folds of his greatcoat. Before she could look again the boy disappeared into the hold. Entering the ship, the men were sent in one direction and the women in another with brisk orders from a young Ensign, "Follow me."

The nurses followed in a line through a maze of hatches and corridors when a sudden stop had them bumping into each other. "Here's your home away from home," the Ensign said, swinging open the door to a tiny cabin. "The head (bathroom) is down there." He pointed to the end of a long passage.

The four nurses stared at the tiny cabin. "Couldn't swing a cat in here," Lt. Marla Jenkins grinned. "But the housekeeping is okay." It was obvious the cabin had been scrubbed clean. Navy blankets were fitted tightly on narrow bunk beds, one above the other.

Brass railings shone with polish and the recently scrubbed floor smelled of disinfectant. Space between the beds was so narrow two people could not pass. There were no portholes as the cabin was beneath the waterline. What the nurses didn't know was that they were lucky to be some distance from the engines. The constant rhythmic rumble meant little sleep for those billeted nearby. One at a time the nurses pushed and shoved their gear beneath the lowest bunks. Marla flipped open the tiny footlocker beneath the sink. "Couldn't hide a camel in here," she joked.

"At least we're not sleeping in hammocks for three weeks," Ruby remarked. Their trip through the companionways took them past the men's sleeping quarters where two by six feet hammocks hung about two feet from the hammocks above. Steel pipes supported the canvas "beds" stretched tightly with ropes. If a man turned over he was likely to bump the nose of the man below.

There were no rules or instructions posted on the cabin walls. Were they confined to quarters or free to go exploring? They were soon to discover that they were limited to an hour on deck for exercise every day, weather permitting. Most sailors believed that a woman on a ship was bad luck.

Right now, with no rules to follow Ruby left the cabin to find the ship's dispensary. In her nurse's uniform no one questioned her presence. After making a dozen wrong turns and getting directions from that many sailors Ruby stepped into a miniature hospital. One room was obviously for sick call where minor ailments were taken care of. Just off this was the surgery with half a dozen bunk beds. Another room held an operating table with bright lights above.

Surgical hardware gleamed in glass-fronted cabinets. An autoclave for sterilizing instruments was ready for use. In one corner a small refrigerator held vital medicines.

A forty-something Captain sat at a desk filling out paperwork when Ruby entered. "Can I help you, Lieutenant?" he asked. As he stretched his six foot four inch frame his head nearly touched the ceiling.

"I was hoping I could help you, Sir," Ruby replied. "I am one of the nurses aboard. Three weeks with nothing to do will have us snapping at each other and anyone who comes near."

Captain Avery nodded. "A lot of the time it's pretty quiet down here. Mostly I see colds, stomach upsets and minor wounds but there are days, especially those after shore leave, when I can use some help. I'll talk to the Captain."

And so the journey began. One day was much like another as the ship sailed past Cuba, through the Panama Canal and continued its slow voyage across the Pacific. In the passing days Ruby and Captain

Avery became good friends and often had heated discussions about the possibility of war in the Pacific.

"I know there is little talk of war at home," the Captain said, "but the signs out here are clear. Japan wants to control the Pacific, not only the smaller islands but Korea, Burma and the Philippines."

Little did the Captain know how right he was. It was only a few months later that Secretary of State Cordell Hull issued a dire warning:

"Vast forces of lawlessness, conquest and destruction are moving across the earth like a savage and dangerous animal at large, and by their very nature those forces will not stop unless and until they recognize that there exists an unbreakable resistance."

Hull's warning was heeded. Throughout 1940 supply ships increased their cargoes bringing food and equipment to the Pacific to be stockpiled in case of war. Military leaders drew up plans to halt invasion of the Philippines by the Japanese. Throughout the coming months transport ships carrying troops and medical personnel would cross the Pacific with destroyers on either side and fighter planes above, a far different trip than the one Ruby was experiencing.

One week into the voyage Ruby returned to quarters after night duty in the dispensary. One sailor missing his footing hit his head on a metal railing. She stayed by his side through the night watching for signs of a concussion.

Standing outside the cabin door she heard rustling sounds, metal hitting metal and strangest of all, YIP! YIP! YIP! Ruby threw open the door. There, on his knees, folding a piece of blanket in the foot locker was the same young Corporal with the moving coat she had seen at embarkation. Wiggling with joy and licking his face was a small brown and white bull terrier. The boy stood up and saluted. "Corporal Johnny Baker Mam," he said.

For the moment Ruby, looking at the soldier and the dog, was at a loss for words.

"This hungry mutt wandered into our training camp," the boy explained, rubbing the dog's ears. "He's not on the roster but he's our good luck charm. We call him Mac, short for MacArthur. We couldn't leave him behind. I've kept him in my locker and he sleeps with me at night but inspections are getting tougher. If the officers find him he might end up in the ocean. Could you please keep him for us?" the boy pleaded.

"He's quiet and won't be any trouble. I'll feed him and clean up after him. They don't inspect your quarters. Your foot locker was the only safe place I could think of to hide him." After this long speech the red-faced soldier was out of breath.

Imagine the surprise of Ruby's three cabin mates when they returned to find Ruby sitting on a lower bunk rubbing the ears of a contented short-tailed terrier. "Meet Mac," Ruby smiled. Seeing the women, the pup put its right paw on its right eyebrow and gave one excited YIP!

"Look! He's saluting," Marla Jenkins laughed. The nurses took turns passing the small dog from one to another while throwing questions at Ruby. "Where did he come from? Who does he belong to? What are we to do with him?" Ruby explained the young soldier's predicament. The vote was unanimous. The nurses would care for Mac until the end of the trip. For the rest of the voyage the footlocker became "Puppy Palace."

A day before reaching Hawaii Ruby was on duty in the dispensary when a young private stumbled in. His face was flushed. He had a runny nose, a non-stop cough and red and watery eyes. Ruby helped the man remove his shirt and popped a thermometer in his mouth. One look at the rosy rash on the soldier's chest and arms and it didn't take a doctor to make a diagnosis. MEASLES! He must have caught them before boarding the ship and had been contagious for days before the rash appeared. Not only was the poor private put in isolation but the entire ship was quarantined. A brief stop in Hawaii for provisions meant no shore leave for either the troops or the nurses.

Weeks later the Island of Guam came into view. The men, there for training purposes, were taken ashore in launches to avoid the coral reefs. Corporal Baker's unit was one of the last to leave the ship. As promised, he left his unit long enough to pick up Mac. Making a mad dash down the corridors, he burst through the cabin door without bothering to knock, flipped open the foot locker, grabbed Mac and dashed off again leaving a "THANKS" echoing in the passage behind him. The women were sorry to see the little dog go and gave the retreating soldier and his pup one last salute.

"I wonder how the Corporal will smuggle Mac ashore?" Ruby mused. "He can't wear a coat in this heat." The nurses never found out.

Ruby asked one of the sailors how much farther it was to Manila. "1300 miles," he replied. Ruby smiled and thought, thirteen hundred more miles and another adventure begins. She had no idea how right she was.

# 3 PARADISE FOUND

"I don't believe it!" Ruby exclaimed as their ship approached Manila Bay. The four nurses stared in astonishment at the sight on the docks below. The screech of the lowering gangplank nearly drowned out the marching notes of "El Capitan" played by a white-uniformed Navy band. Crowds of locals who considered "boat days" as days of celebration jammed the area. The smell of copra (coconut drying in the sun) hovered over the docks. The nurses with gear in tow joined the remaining military on board in a line down the narrow ramp.

"Aaiiee!" Marla, whose eyes were on a young Lieutenant, tripped and missed a grab at the rail. In a flash Ruby dropped her gear, hooked Marla under the arm pulling her back from a certain dip in the bay. The embarrassed nurse glanced down to see a laughing crowd. Without further mishap the nurses walked to the end of the gangway to meet a straight-faced Colonel waiting there.

"Welcome to the Philippines," the Colonel said, having trouble hiding a grin. "The Corporal will take you first to Sternberg and will drop your gear off at the nurses' quarters." Again the women were in for a surprise. Instead of the usual jeep the Colonel pointed to a shiny tan four-door sedan. One by one they handed their gear to the Corporal who stowed it in the trunk.

The drive to Sternberg Hospital in the busy center of Manila was an eye-opener. The air was fragrant with the perfume of the china roses and orchids from the walled gardens along the coast. Heading down Dewey Boulevard the driver slowed for small ponies pulling two wheeled carts. Small shops grew in number like mushrooms and red cobblestone streets gave way to paved boulevards as they approached the heart of the city. Ruby watched cars fighting each other for position in the narrow streets. Sidewalks teemed with people moving in and out of dozens of shops both small and large. A Spanish style cathedral loomed ahead as beautiful as any found in Europe. Soon the 450 bed Sternberg Hospital, a complex of two-story Spanish style buildings came into view. The sedan pulled up to the main entrance and the nurses piled out.

"Just check at the desk for directions to the head nurses' office," the Corporal said opening the door for the women. "Wow," Ruby exclaimed entering the pristine lobby. Shining floors had obviously received a lot of attention. Pale green walls offered a soothing effect to patients and families. A half dozen people crowded around the reception area. The nurses got in line.

"Second floor, first door to the right," a harried Private behind the counter told them without glancing up.

The name on the door was Captain Maude Davison, the head administrator of the Army Nurse Corps in the Philippines. A busy Lieutenant at a well-worn desk pointed to four straight-backed chairs and instructed them to wait. Ten minutes went by, twenty minutes, thirty minutes. When the door finally swung open the nurses entered a Spartan office. The beige walls held no pictures. There were no flowers on the simple desk. Two grey metal filing cabinets stood at attention opposite the desk. The shiny bare floor was never intended for the click clack of high heels. Three straight-back bamboo chairs looked so uncomfortable that Ruby was certain that visitors would not stay long.

Almost hidden behind the desk sat a small sharp-featured, grey-haired woman. Her back was as straight as the starched uniform that refused to let it bend. "Welcome to Sternberg," she barked with a quick salute then held out her hand. It was obvious that no reply was expected as the four nurses silently returned the salute and handed over their orders.

"There are five Army hospitals on the Islands," she told the nurses. "Everyone is run by the book.

There are no excuses for missing or being late to a shift. You will wear proper attire at all times while on duty. You will follow the instructions of the doctors to the letter whether or not you agree with them. Understood?" The four nodded, again without saying a word.

Captain Davison stamped their papers. "Come," she called at a rap on the door. The nurses turned to see a tall, big-boned woman. Lieutenant Josie Nesbit, nicknamed "Mama Josie" by the Filipina nurses. Her soft hazel eyes were framed with wire rimmed glasses. An unruly strand of light brown hair escaped from under her cap. She welcomed the newcomers with an easy smile. Marla let out a quiet sigh of relief. A breath of fresh air had entered the room.

"Lieutenant Nesbit will assist you in locating your assignments," Maude Davison said, handing the Lieutenant the nurses' orders. Josie Nesbit was the second in command at Sternberg. It was she who set the schedules and made the duty assignments.

"Follow me," she smiled at the new arrivals. One in particular caught her eye. Ruby looked up with eyes thoughtful and serene. *'Here is one,'* Josie Nesbit thought, *'worth watching. She will never let the world make her miserable. There's a toughness there under that quiet smile.'*

Following the Lieutenant through Sternberg Hospital, Ruby was impressed. She saw a hospital as modern as any in the States. She walked past separate wards for officers and enlisted men, a large, well equipped laboratory, as well as surgical, and obstetrical suites. She peeked in a busy X-ray department with patients in wheelchairs and on gurneys waiting their turn. Every room showed signs of vigorous cleaning. Ruby was soon to learn that all of the Army hospitals on the islands met the highest standards. Captain Maude Davison would accept nothing less.

The nurses followed Lieutenant Nesbit from ward to ward. After a quick hug and "See you at the nurses' quarters," each was delivered to meet the staff at her new assignment, all but Ruby. Keeping up with the quick pace she followed the Lieutenant to the ground floor and out the door where a driver was waiting in a jeep. The top part of her gear stuck out from the back. "Your new orders," Josie Nesbit said handing her more papers. "The driver will take you to the launches at Manila Bay. Good luck."

Glancing down at the orders Ruby saw she would not be working at Sternberg. Neither would she be at Fort McKinley, seven miles from Manila or Fort Stotsenburg in the north near Clark Field. She was to report to the station hospital at Fort Mills on the small, hilly island of Corregidor. Unknown to Ruby, the two square mile rocky island would play a key role in the coming defense of the Philippines.

For the remainder of 1940, Ruby truly lived in a paradise. Soft ocean winds kept the island six to ten degrees cooler than the mainland. The comfortable nurses' quarters were furnished with beautifully crafted bamboo chairs, tables and beds. A screened veranda was ideal for early morning breakfast or evening meals. Covered porches led to a small courtyard.

Ruby fell quickly into the routine of four-hour day shifts and eight-hour night shifts. Her competence in the operating room again made her a favorite with the surgeons. Most cases were routine whether a simple appendectomy or a more complicated removal of a gall bladder. Critical cases were sent to Sternberg. Just as she had at Walter Reed, when on ward duty, Ruby became a favorite with the patients. Her reassuring presence and her sense of humor kept temperament low and morale high. In addition, her superiors were well aware of her uncanny ability to spot trouble before it became a full-blown emergency.

When not on duty Ruby found dozens of ways to use her free time. Launches ran between Corregidor and Manila Bay like taxis. The thirty-mile trip took about an hour. On days off Ruby rummaged through busy shops seeking handmade crafts for her family. Watching all of the buying and selling going on Ruby shook her head remembering her shipboard conversations with Captain Jenkins. His warnings of war in the Pacific had to be wrong. In 1940 this thriving City of Manila showed no signs of preparing for war.

Little did Ruby know that while she shopped for gifts, Japanese factory workers were on overtime turning out guns and planes. While Ruby joined three other nurses for doubles at tennis, Japanese shipyard workers were on double time. As Ruby watched ball games between rival Companies, Japanese troops were issued summer uniforms and trained for jungle fighting and amphibious assaults. While Ruby relaxed after work at the officer's club, Japanese spies were infiltrating all areas Japan planned to conquer. The information gained allowed them to bring maps up to date and to discover defense plans.

At the same time, right under Ruby's nose, trucks loaded with food and equipment moved in and out of Malinta Tunnel on Corregidor where a stockpile of emergency supplies grew larger each day. This underground fortress would become General MacArthur's headquarters should the Japanese attack.

At the end of her morning shift on the 13th of February 1941 Ruby was handed new orders along with a note from Captain Davison. "Your work here has been exemplary," Captain Davison wrote. "We are assigning you as surgical and head nurse for the station hospital at Camp John Hay. You will leave tomorrow with the supply trucks."

Camp John Hay! If the Philippines was every nurse's dream, Camp John Hay, three miles from Baguio City, was the frosting on the cake. Two hundred miles north of Manila in northern Luzon, Baguio City rested at the foot of the Cordillera Mountains. The locals called it the summer capital of the Philippines and rightly so for it boasted a magnificent summer palace with Buckingham style gates, beautiful gardens and well manicured lawns. With a climate cooler than Manila it was a perfect spot for rest and recreation.

The sun was peeking over the tips of Corregidor's hills when Ruby met her driver for the trip north. "Happy Valentine's day, Mam," the Sergeant greeted Ruby as she climbed up to sit beside him. Ruby had forgotten all about the holiday. It was February 14th, the first day of an adventure Ruby would never forget.

Bumps and bruises were frequent as the lumbering supply truck rumbled over an uneven road.

There were deep ruts, now dry, where other heavy trucks left their tracks during the rainy season. A wild pig crossing the primitive road brought the truck to a screeching halt. The sudden jolt threw Ruby forward toward the windshield when a strong arm shot out pulling her back.

"Sorry, Mam," the driver apologized.

"Thanks, Sergeant," Ruby gasped, catching her breath. "I'll take one well intended whack over a battered face any day."

Now and then they passed small villages of nipa huts. Houses on stilts dotted the nearby foothills. Ruby smiled at tiny naked children chasing chickens in the narrow streets. Several miles beyond one village a noisy toucan with a brightly colored bill scolded Ruby and the driver. Perched high on a pine branch its loud screech ordered the intruders to move on. A trip that could be made in six hours in the dry season took twice that long after heavy rains.

A deep purple twilight slid down the mountains when the driver at last delivered a bumped and bruised Ruby to the small station hospital. Waiting on the steps in the cool evening air was a plump, rosy-cheeked nurse in fatigues with rolled up sleeves. Her hair was brownish, short and straight. Her impish grin immediately put Ruby at ease. She jumped up the minute the truck pulled up. Military protocol was forgotten.

"Boy, am I glad to see you," the girl shouted embracing Ruby in a bear hug. "Lieutenant Beatrice Chambers at your service but call me Bea. And this is Ching." She rubbed the ears of a friendly mutt that was half chow and half something else. His fur looked as if he had a khaki shirt on over a brown coat. "The G.I.s got him as a watch dog but he spends most of his time curled up on the porch of the nurses' quarters. Shake hands with the lady, Ching."

Ruby reached out and took the paw of the wiggling pooch. The dog jumped up and licked her face.

"He's telling you, 'Welcome to the best hospital on the islands'. Well, if we're not the best at least we are the smallest."

Nurse Bea continued non-stop. "One doctor, two nurses, that's you and me, and thirty four beds, six occupied at the moment. We're on twenty-four hour duty with eight hour shifts and on-call the rest of the time. Usually the casualties are something minor like being hit with a golf ball. Now and then we can expect an automobile accident, usually not serious as well as the normal run of appendices. Sometimes Doctor Jacobs relieves us for a couple of hours. When that happens I'll take you up the mountain to pick orchids." The young nurse ran out of breath.

"You must know this whole area well," Ruby remarked.

"I should," Bea answered. "I got my nurse's training in the States but I was born near here. My father owned and operated a mine in the mountains. Both my parents are gone now but the family still owns the mines."

"How long have you been on duty?" Ruby asked.

"Forty-eight hours, but we have trained corpsmen to help. Some are so good they could do the operations alone. Of course, Dr. Jacobs would never permit such a thing. Most operations are done by civilian doctors from Baguio."

"Night duty is mine tonight," Ruby insisted. "Show me the nurses' quarters. I'll throw my stuff on a cot, wash my face and come right back."

"But I'll need to show you where things are and bring you up to date on the patients," Bea protested.

"I'll take care of that." A screen door that needed oiling opened revealing short, stocky Captain Eugene Jacobs, the hospital C. O.. Loose strands of dark hair flecked with gray fell over shrewd and intelligent eyes. He gave Ruby a quick salute followed by a firm handshake. "You will never get a better welcome than here," he told Ruby. "Lieutenant Chambers has been working non-stop since the last nurse's tour of duty ended."

"Lieutenant Chambers, get some sleep," he ordered. "Lieutenant Bradley, follow me."

The doctor led Ruby from bed to bed pointing out the charts and the supply cabinets, at the same time sounding like a travel agent for Baguio. "A great city," he said, "with plenty of open air markets where you can find everything you need and to top it off we are only twenty miles from the white sand beaches, the stately palms and the golden sun of Lingayen Gulf." The doctor went on to assure Ruby that her assignment was one of the best the army could give. At least, that was what the military thought at the time. They were unaware that Lingayen Gulf was ideal for landings by enemy forces.

Ruby's first night at the hospital was a quiet one. It was a good thing for she was worn out from being tossed around like a ping pong ball on the two hundred mile trip to Camp John Hay. She made simple notes on each patient. A few required temperature checks and there was an occasional call for water. After a twelve hour shift Ruby found the sun pouring down the green and yellow mountains a welcome sight.

"Morning!" a cheerful and rested Bea Chambers popped through the squeaky screen door. "Anything I should know? If not, go and get some shut-eye. You'll need to check your bed for iguanas. Sometimes they get in and they have a fondness for clean sheets. Oh, and get rid of the white uniform. You're in the jungle now. I left fatigues on your cot. Hope you can sew. You'll have to cut them down a bit."

Back in the nurses' quarters Ruby looked with dismay at two size 44 fatigues. It was the only size the army issued and intended for a man twice Ruby's size. Her other possessions were scattered on the floor. She picked up her toothbrush, her scissors and her soap. Were the locals going through her things looking for valuables? Nothing seemed to be missing. She yawned. She'd ask Bea about it after she got some shut-eye. The room was warm. She opened a window with a missing screen and curled up on her cot. Within minutes she was asleep.

Four hours later Ruby awakened to a thumping and an excited chattering. She opened one eye to discover a family of monkeys. Coming down from their mountain trees the curious monkeys climbed through the open window and made themselves at home. One large male held Ruby's shoe. Another waved her scissors and the third was eating her soap. Squinting through half closed eyes Ruby was so fascinated watching them that it never occurred to her to call for help. Fortunately, it wasn't necessary. Within minutes two young corpsmen hearing the noise came through the door with a large mosquito net. With a loud squeal the two smaller monkeys scampered out the window.

The corpsmen approached the large male who backed away and bared his teeth. With practiced skill they tossed the net over the furious animal. Still holding Ruby's shoe, it struggled and screeched, lunging while trying to bite the hands securing the net. The corpsmen held tight. There was no escape.

"What will you do with him?" Ruby asked watching the boys carry the furious creature out the door. It was still holding her shoe but she could lose a hand trying to get it back.

"We will turn him loose in the mountains. Meanwhile, keep your window closed until we get a new screen. Supposed to be some on that supply truck."

Within two days Ruby learned how changeable the Baguio weather was. Early in the morning she wore a sweater with the fatigues. By ten o'clock she shed the sweater and rolled up her sleeves. By three o'clock a chilly fog rolled in and she put on the sweater again. By evening there was a fire in the fireplace and blankets. When it rained it looked like a gallon of water poured down at one time.

As the days and months passed hospital case loads increased. Patients arrived from the lumber camps high in the mountains and the gold mining camps below Baguio. Most were Americans working in the Philippines. Civilian doctors and surgeons from the town helped out when the emergency room was overcrowded.

In addition to the usual injuries and illnesses, the accident rate increased during the rainy season. For nearly six months from May to October the sun didn't shine. It rained twenty-four hours a day. One morning in mid August when the clouds parted, a joker put up a sign, "WHAT YOU SEE TODAY IS THE SUN!"

By December the rainy season passed. It was a sunny Sunday morning when Ruby set out to walk to church. With a brisk stride and arms swinging she was halfway there when a steady drone of low flying aircraft caught her attention. She looked up to see painted on the wings and fuselage the emblem of the rising sun. There was no mistake. These were Japanese planes!

There had been little talk of war in the Pacific. Yet Ruby recalled the ship doctor's words: "I know there is no talk of war at home, but the signs out here are clear. Japan wants to control the Pacific, not only the smaller islands but Korea, Burma and the Philippines as well." Was this a prophecy come true?

Ruby looked at shuttered storefronts for the nearest shelter. She raced up the rickety steps to the porch of a small hotel. She stood in the shadows watching and breathed a sigh of relief when the last plane was out of sight. *Surely this wasn't a sign of coming hostilities*, she thought. Camp John Hay, a

Filipino training camp, was a threat to no one. Yet, Ruby wondered why large shipments of tetanus serum arrived at the hospital in the past week. One thing that led to tetanus was an open wound.

Ruby scanned the sky once more making sure the planes were out of sight. Entering the church late she heard the minister talking about living in tense times. The congregation was soon to find out how right he was.

# 4 THE ATTACK

On December 7, 1941, two nurses were beginning their day. In Hawaii Lieutenant Ruth Erickson, a Navy nurse, chatted at breakfast with other Navy nurses before reporting for duty.

5299 miles away at Camp John Hay in the Philippines, Ruby Bradley hummed a tune as she left the hospital supply room pushing open the door with one elbow. Her arms were loaded with surgical packs. Because the Philippines are beyond International Dateline, that same day was December 8th at Camp John Hay.

Lieutenant Ruth Erickson tells what happened next in Hawaii.

"It was 7:55 a.m. Two or three of us were sitting in the dining room Sunday morning having a late breakfast and talking over coffee. Suddenly we heard planes roaring overhead and we said, The 'fly boys' are really busy at Ford Island this morning."

The island was directly across the channel from the hospital. We didn't think too much about it since the reserves were often there for weekend training. We no sooner got those words out when we started to hear noises that were foreign to us.

I leaped out of my chair and dashed to the nearest window in the corridor. Right then there was a plane flying directly over the top of our quarters, a one-story structure. The rising sun under the wing of the plane denoted the enemy. Had I known the pilot, one could almost see his features around his goggles. He was obviously saving his ammunition for the ships. Just down the row, all the ships were sitting there--the [battleships] California (BB-44), the Arizona (BB-39), the Oklahoma (BB-37), and others.

My heart was racing, the telephone was ringing, the chief nurse, Gertrude Arnest, was saying, "Girls, get into your uniforms at once, This is the real thing!"

I was in my room by that time changing into uniform. It was getting dusky, almost like evening. Smoke was rising from burning ships.

I dashed across the street, through a shrapnel shower, got into the lanai and just stood still for a second as were a couple of doctors. I felt like I was frozen to the ground, but it was only a split second. I ran to the orthopedic dressing room but it was locked. A corpsmen ran to the OD's [Officer-of-the-Day's] desk for the keys. It seemed like an eternity before he returned and the room was opened. We drew water into every container we could find and set up the instrument boiler. Fortunately, we still had electricity and water. Dr. [CDR Clyde W.] Brunson, the chief of medicine was making a sick call when the bombing started.

The first patient came into our dressing room at 8:25 a.m. with a large opening in his abdomen and bleeding profusely. They started an intravenous and transfusion. I can still see the tremor of Dr. Brunson's hand as he picked up the needle. Everyone was terrified. The patient died within the hour.

Then the burned patients streamed in. The USS Nevada (BB-36) had managed some steam and attempted to get out of the channel. They were unable to make it and went aground on Hospital Point right near the hospital. There was heavy oil on the water and the men dived off the ship and swam through these waters to Hospital Point, not too great a distance except when one is burned. How they ever managed, I'll never know. The tropical dress at the time was white t-shirts and shorts. The burns began where the pants ended. Burned arms and faces were plentiful.

Personnel retrieved a supply of flit guns from stock. We filled these with tannic acid to spray burned bodies. Then we gave these gravely injured patients sedatives for their intense pain.

Orthopedic patients were eased out of their beds with no time for linen changes as an unending stream of burn patients continued until mid afternoon. A doctor, who several days before had renal surgery and was still convalescing, got out of his bed and began to assist the other doctors.

About 12 noon the galley personnel came around with sandwiches and cold drinks; we ate on the run. About 2 o'clock the chief nurse was making rounds to check on all the units and arrange relief schedules. I was relieved around 4 p.m. and went over to the nurses' quarters where everything was intact. I freshened up, had something to eat, and went back on duty at 8 p.m. I was scheduled to report to a surgical unit.

By now it was dark and we worked with flashlights. The maintenance people and anyone else who could manage a hammer and nails were putting up black drapes or black paper to seal the crevices against any light that might stream to the outside. Who knew when the next attack would come?"

At the same moment Ruth Erickson was dodging shrapnel and machine gun fire in Hawaii, at Camp John Hay Ruby Bradley loaded the autoclave with surgical instruments. To avoid infection all instruments had to be sterile and one of Ruby's jobs was to see that they were.

A civilian surgeon would soon arrive for the first operation of the day. One thing that puzzled Ruby was the over abundance of supplies. In the adjoining room, surgical packs were piled to the ceiling and more were delivered from Manila every month. How could they possibly have a need for all those surgical packs? Within the hour she would find out.

That same morning Dr. Jacobs relaxed in his office finishing his second cup of coffee. His thoughts were interrupted by a tap on the door. "Enter," he called. A young orderly handed the doctor a message. The words were brief. "Report to headquarters immediately." The orderly looked upset but Dr. Jacobs had no time to find out why. On his way out he stuck his head in the operating room. "The Colonel has called a powwow of all officers. I'll see what this is all about," he told Ruby. "Back in a few minutes." The Colonel was John Horan, Commanding Officer of Camp John Hay.

Dr. Jacobs stepped out in a yard cracked and baked by the hot sun. He gave a sigh of relief. Fortunately jackets weren't required in this heat. Short and stocky with an athletic build he usually walked the short distance to headquarters but the message had a sense of urgency he could not ignore. His sporty 1938 Chevy was in the nearest lot. He hopped in, turned the key and roared off, reaching headquarters in minutes. He didn't bother to look for a place to park but left the car in front of the main entrance. The quartermaster pulling up right behind him did the same.

The minute the two entered the building they sensed something terrible had happened. The cheery hellos they expected were absent. The front desk was empty. Lt. Velasco who usually greeted visitors with a joke was nowhere to be seen. A low murmur of sounds led them in to the Ready Room. They paused in the doorway to see a crowd of stunned officers gathered around a radio. The news coming from Station KZRH in Manila carried across the room. What they heard was unbelievable. The announcer was relaying word by word a message coming directly from Hawaii.

The stupefied announcer was half shouting, half crying. "Pearl Harbor is under attack. The Japanese are hitting ships at anchor with everything they've got! Waves of enemy planes are attacking. It's terrible. It's horrible. Ship after ship is going down. Men in the water are fighting for their lives." The announcer had difficulty getting the words out between his tears.

The officers were so intent on listening that they did not notice Colonel Horan enter the room until he spoke. "For months we have speculated about Japan's intentions and the possibility of war. Why else have they been taking scrap iron and raw materials from the Philippines over the past years? I doubt that we are in immediate danger. The last place to expect a raid is on a Filipino training camp. The Japanese who live in this area know that our only weapons are World War One rifles. However, we are the nearest U.S. Base to Japan. The Japanese could attack just to show the world how powerful they are at the moment. We would be foolish not to be prepared."

The officers looked at each other in disbelief. An air attack wasn't the only thing to be concerned about. Each was thinking the words that the Colonel had not said. Camp John Hay was only twenty miles away from Lingayen Gulf, an ideal spot for landing enemy troops.

Like bullets from a gun Colonel Horan shot out rapid orders. "Capt. Jacobs, return to the hospital and ready your staff for emergencies. Lt. Warner, assemble all Japanese civilians and bring them into camp. House them in our two deserted barracks. Set up a rotation of guards. Lt. Velasco, collect a crew and build an eight foot fence around the barracks."

Colonel Horan continued with one order after another as Dr. Jacobs left on the run to his car. He was glad he had parked by Headquarters entrance. In no time he reached the hospital. He took the steps two at a time shouting as he reached the door, "Lieutenants Bradley and Chambers, my office!"

Bea was bathing a little girl who had been kicked by a carabao. Her broken leg was healing nicely. Bea grabbed a towel and quickly dried the child, pulling a small gown over her head. "Back in a jiffy," she smiled. "Don't do any dances while I'm gone."

Ruby dropped the surgical packs on a nearby table and took off on a run.

The two curious nurses entered the cluttered office to find the usually unflappable doctor slamming his fist against his desk with such force that one corner splintered. He turned to the women. "The Japanese are bombing Pearl Harbor. We could be hit at any time." The nurses were speechless. No sooner had he spit out the words, than they heard a faint drone of approaching planes. The drone grew to a roar leaving their ears ringing. The rumble of engines carried to the rafters shaking the building. Ignoring the danger the three ran to the window to see eighteen Japanese twin-engine bombers overhead. The planes were flying so close to the buildings that Ruby could see the pilots' faces.

One after another the terror birds dipped low. Finding their targets, they delivered their deadly payloads. Thirty, forty, fifty or more bombs split the earth... tearing, gashing, gouging. A screech from the sky like a giant banshee was followed by an enormous burst of smoke and earth near the officers' quarters. Huge billows of dirt and dust covered the Post like a dirty blanket. Along with the smell of powder, smoke rolled up stinging their eyes. Would the next bomb be a direct hit? The dust was so thick it made breathing difficult. Ruby and Bea rushed to the wards to be with their terrified patients.

Dust covered the floor, beds, tables and linens. Bea raced to close windows while Ruby and the corpsmen moved from bed to bed tying on face masks for protection and placing those patients who could be moved under their beds.

Just as they arrived without warning, the drone of the engines faded away. The ten-minute attack left those on the ground stunned with disbelief. The nurses and corpsmen moved from bed to bed calming frightened patients and returning those who had been moved to their beds. Dust-covered sheets were replaced with new ones. Fortunately the hospital was not touched but glancing out the door Ruby shuddered to see pieces of a 1938 Chevy in a gaping thirty foot crater. If the doctor had been five minutes later he would have been hit.

A worried Dr. Jacobs issued orders. He was a medical doctor, not a surgeon yet surgical skills would be most needed in the next few hours. "Lt. Bradley, check the autoclave, gather as many surgical packs as you can. Lt. Chambers, assess the casualties as they come in. Minor wounds can wait."

Ruby ran to the operating room. She breathed a sigh of relief. The hospital still had electricity. This was what she was trained for. With calm efficiency she laid scalpels and hemostats in the autoclave. Within minutes they would be sterilized and ready for use. But the medical team did not have minutes as the corpsmen carried in the first litter.

On the outskirts of Baguio a young mother, Susan Dudley, chose this beautiful Sunday morning to take her one year old for a walk. As she strolled in the shade of the tall pines she had no way to know that this quiet morning would turn deadly. She looked up, a curious expression on her face as she heard the first faint drone of aircraft. *Our planes are out early today*, she thought.

The first bomb smashed to pieces a small nipa hut yards away. Susan screamed. Holding her child so tightly he protested, she searched frantically for shelter. She was on the open road. There were no buildings on either side. The flat surface offered no ditch as a hiding place. The roar of the planes grew louder as more and more dealers of death filled the sky. The second bomb fell. Susan and her son dodged a direct hit but not soon enough.

As the last of the bombers disappeared from sight, nervous neighbors found the young mother and her son semi-conscious at the side of the dirt road. Blood poured from open wounds in the woman's legs. An old woman collected scarves from onlookers and wrapped them around the legs to stop the flow of blood. The baby was silent with a blue cast to his lips.

The old woman pointed to the crowd. "Hospital," she croaked.

Two young Filipino boys retrieved a door from a damaged hut. Gently they lifted the mother still clinging to her baby and placed her on the make-shift litter. With short, quick steps they carried the two to the hospital.

A quick examination by Bea sent Susan to the operating room. Dr. Jacobs shook his head as he studied her injuries. His first task was to stop the bleeding. Susan's leg wounds were so severe there was no chance of saving the right leg. Yet, she held on to her son so tightly that Ruby had to pry her fingers away to lift the child from his mother's arms.

It was evident the little one was in trouble. He lay perfectly still, not uttering a sound. His obvious injury was a shattered kneecap but worse than that his blue lips signaled that he was in severe shock.

"We'll have to rush through this," the doctor muttered. "We'll be getting other casualties. You see to the baby, I'll see to the mother."

Ruby began artificial respiration but there was no response. She opened the child's mouth to give him gentle breaths of air but still no response. She grabbed an oxygen mask and put it over the baby's mouth. There was not a single breath or a cry. "Do you think we could put some Adrenalin in his heart?" Ruby called out to the doctor.

"If you want to do it go ahead," the Doctor called from the other room.

Ruby got a syringe and looked at the long needle. She looked at the baby. This was not part of her training. What if she missed the heart and hit an artery? The child could bleed to death. It was too risky. She couldn't do it. She glanced at the medicine cabinet. There was a bottle of whiskey on the bottom shelf. On another cart she spied the sugar bowl standing next to the coffee pot.

Growing up on a farm Ruby remembered many of the home remedies her mother used. She picked up some gauze, made a small sack out of it and filled it with sugar. She unscrewed the cap on the whiskey bottle and poured a hefty amount of whiskey over the sugar sack. She put the small sack in the baby's mouth. It was then a near miracle happened. The baby sucked that whiskey-soaked sugar sack like everything and within five minutes he was as pink as a rose and yelling his head off.

From the next room his mother was moaning and crying. "Where's my baby? Where's my baby?"

Doctor Jacobs replied. "Well, you hear him in there. He's going to be all right. Now our job is to take care of you."

He turned his attention back to his patient thankful that the daily workouts he was often teased about would give him the stamina he needed in the hours to come. His greatest concern was his lack of surgical experience. As an intern he had assisted at operations but that was many years ago. *You are a doctor,* he told himself. *This woman needs your help now and you are the only one here to give it.* He straightened his shoulders and snapped on his surgical gloves.

"Lieutenant Bradley," he called. "I need your help."

Ruby left the pink-faced howling child in the care of a corpsman, grabbed her surgical gown and worked with the doctor on what was to be the first of thirty-seven operations performed in the hours to come.

The arrival of the wounded began with a trickle that turned into a flood. A hotel that served as a rest camp for soldiers was hit and two of them were wounded. Standing by a door one of them was thrown back through two doors and hit his head against them. The other had a long splinter of wood that went into his thigh about eight or ten inches and had to be removed. These injuries were easily handled but neither Dr. Jacobs nor the nurses had any previous experience in taking care of the severely wounded patients who followed.

The serious injuries arrived one after another brought in by cars, trucks, wagons, donkey carts and almost anything on wheels. Beds filled rapidly. Litters lined the corridors. Bea and the corpsmen worked frantically to assess the severity of the injuries as more and more wounded arrived on makeshift litters.

Dr. Jacobs stepped out for a moment between surgeries to change his sweat-soaked scrubs. "Everybody listen to me," he told Bea and the corpsmen. "These patients are all bleeding. We've got to stop the bleeding right now! Elevate extremities. Use anything you can get to stop the bleeding! Tourniquets! Compression bandages! Hemostats! Even your fingers, if they are clean. Bring all bad cases to the operating room."

"Eugene, looks like you could use some help," a gray haired lady called out. Dr. Eugene Jacobs looked up, and heaved a great sigh of relief. Tiny Dr. Beulah Allen, the Quartermaster's wife and a retired surgeon stood framed in the doorway surveying the chaos. "Looks like these folks need a bit of fixing up."

Never was a sight so welcome as this no nonsense woman with pixie features and short-clipped hair. Retired she might be but she had not forgotten her training or her surgical skills.

"Take your pick, Beulah," a relieved Dr. Jacobs waved his hand over the wounded.

For the next thirty-two hours, working non-stop Dr. Jacobs and Ruby assisted the skilled lady surgeon saving one life after another. Less difficult cases Dr. Jacobs handled alone. Occasionally when a stray Jap plane dropped a bomb or two, surgery stopped. If possible the patient was moved to a safer place, sometimes under the operating table. Surgery resumed again when the plane moved on. "Guess they want to let us know the war is still on," Ruby muttered.

The day turned to night. The autoclave hummed hour after hour. Ruby lost count of the times she removed one set of instruments and put another set in its place. By late night the flood of wounded trickled to a stream. Still, there was no rest for the doctors. Lights came on while the medical team worked. As Ruby set up and assisted in one operation after another Bea took over the post-op care. At the end of thirty-seven surgeries Dr. Jacobs, Dr. Allen, Ruby and Bea collapsed on nearby chairs for a well deserved break. The work was far from over. Those with less serious injuries still needed attention.

"What I don't understand," Dr. Jacobs mused, "is where are our American planes? We are only 100 miles from Clark Field."

No one at Camp John Hay was aware that the previous night the B-17 bombers and P-40 fighters from Clark Field spent long hours patrolling the skies over the islands. On the morning of December 8th, the returning planes lined up in neat rows on the tarmac waiting their turn for refueling. News had just arrived at Clark Field of the bombing of Pearl Harbor. Flight crews worked at top speed to ready the planes for flight. The pilots, who needed a break, chowed down their first meal of the day in the mess hall. They had not yet received the news of the bombing of Camp John Hay.

At the same time, following the attack on Baguio the Japanese planes flew directly to Clark Air Field and Fort Stotsenburg. They could not have wished for a more perfect target than the one they found. Like birds of prey Japanese bombers shook the earth dropping their deadly payload on row after row of unmanned planes. Flames shot from the roofs of buildings hit by the barrage of bombs. With a whoosh and a roar the hospital building collapsed. The destruction was so great that fire crews faced tough decisions as to what, if anything, could be saved.

Men who grabbed their rifles soon realized that shooting at the planes was as useless as hitting an elephant with a pellet gun. Their own planes which could have offered resistance littered the tarmac. Nothing was left but burned out hulks. Direct hits on fuel trucks triggered more explosions with sheets of flame shooting across the sky creating a bizarre Fourth of July spectacular.

Watching the last wave of bombers disappear across the mountains, soldiers and civilians plunged into the haze of smoke to answer the cries of the wounded. A shout echoed across the field. "LOOK OUT!" Before the men reached their comrades a new wave of Japanese Zeros filled the sky buzzing like angry wasps. Diving low with machine guns blazing they sprayed the field bringing more death and destruction. In one terrible hour the Japanese destroyed almost all of the U.S. airpower in the Philippines. Only seven planes were left untouched.

# 5 ESCAPE

In talking with a friend and fellow nurse, Mardell Cottle, Col. Ruby Bradley recalled the surprise bombing of Camp John Hay.

"After the surprise attack on the Philippines by the Japanese the war in the Philippines was on. I felt that I was living a charmed life. December 8th the summer Capital was the first place to be attacked by Japanese planes. Bombs fell all around the hospital but no direct hits on the building. Thirty-seven soldiers were killed, many injured. Then the roads leading to the hospital were bombed minutes after. Lucky was the password. For the next two weeks it was a constant run to the air raid shelters, near hits by

50 lb. bombs, many were duds. Had more the bombs been active the camp would have been lost. There were many instances of danger but one becomes accustomed to danger."

From December 8th to December 23rd danger WAS the by-word. With every hospital bed taken there was little chance for uninterrupted sleep for Ruby or Bea. Ruby was curled up on her cot after a sixteen-hour shift when a banging on her window brought her upright. Had the enemy arrived? Ruby was angry. She had had enough of bombings and injuries. She needed sleep!

She hopped out of bed and felt around in the dark for a weapon. The golf club in the corner was better than nothing. She grabbed it with both hands and swung it over her shoulder ready to clobber the night visitor. She reached up and whipped back the curtains to see the grinning face of the monkey thief happily tapping her stolen shoe against the window.

"GO AWAY! GO AWAY! SCAT!" Ruby yelled brandishing the golf club. Her visitor bobbed its head, bared its teeth, then hopped down dropping the shoe in the bushes below. Without a backward glance it scampered away on all fours heading for the nearest tree. Too tired to retrieve her shoe, an exhausted Ruby went back to bed.

In the days that followed the first attack there was little rest for anyone. Occasional bombers dropped their payload on Camp John Hay one day and on the next flew to create more havoc at Clark Field. With both naval and air forces destroyed there was nothing to stop them. The Camp was fortunate that many of the bombs were duds and casualties were light.

On December 10th Ruby moving from bed to bed in the ward was startled by a grinning red-haired man who popped his head in the door. He had a long, lean build and a boyish face red from the sun. His civilian clothes tagged him as one of the mining engineers. "Murphy at your service, Mam." He put his head back and laughed out loud. "No more problems with bombs. My men dug a tunnel thirty feet back into the hillside. You just skip over there when you hear the planes."

"Thanks, Murphy," Ruby called out with a wave knowing she would stay with her patients no matter how many bombs fell.

For two weeks rumors flew about the camp like feathers in the wind. Some said they were moving out. Scouts in the hills reported 84 Japanese ships anchored in Lingayen Bay. On December 12th the first Japanese troops hit the beaches. It was only a matter of days before enemy soldiers would overrun the camp.

The rumors proved to be true. On December 21st Captain Jacobs handed Ruby and Bea new orders. "We are moving patients and large equipment today to Notre Dame Hospital in Baguio. We will evacuate the camp in two days and try to reach Manila." Along with the orders he handed both women combat boots. "Wear these, there will be a lot of climbing. Take with you only absolute necessities. I'll be damned if we are the first Americans captured!"

Shortly before the sun rose on December 23rd the camp was on the move. The mountains cast deep shadows over the hospital as troops loaded trucks and set fire to anything the Japanese might find useful. The Japanese civilians confined to two barracks laid out a large Japanese flag on the ground so the bombers might avoid them. They quietly rejoiced that they would soon be free.

In their quarters Ruby and Bea tried on the combat boots. "I could put both feet in one of these," Ruby laughed. The oversize boots were so uncomfortable she tossed them aside. Both nurses put on leggings with their oldest pair of duty shoes so their feet would be up to the long walk ahead.

"Wait," Ruby said. "I need to take care of something." In a flash she was gone, dashing up the hospital steps and making straight for the supply room. Suppose they returned within a few days or a week? There were things they must have. Who knew what emergencies they would meet?

From the few supplies remaining Ruby chose the bone instruments and wrapped each one separately with a few heliostats and retractors. After assisting Drs. Jacobs and Allen in 37 operations that first day she knew these were needed for the most likely injuries. She looked around for a hiding place. The big box in the corner would do. Leaving the box empty she slid the life-saving instruments behind it. Not the best spot but there was no time to find another.

Returning to the nurses' quarters Ruby helped Bea fill a knapsack with any food they could find, tins of salmon were tossed in along with smoked sausage, crackers, coffee, corn meal, sugar and salt. At the last minute Bea threw in a box of candy. Another knapsack held a dress and sweater for each and a few personal items.

"What was that?" Bea exclaimed. The two abandoned their food search to listen. Rifle fire in the distance sounded like popping rivets from a steel tank. The Japanese troops were at the door of Camp John Hay. Echoing in the hills the nurses heard explosions, one after another. Desperate Filipino troops were blowing bridges and mountain passes to halt the Japanese advance.

"On the double," Captain Jacobs shouted.

The nurses grabbed the knapsacks and flew out the door.

"Where's Ching?" Bea asked looking around for her pet?

"Probably took off for the mountains when the first bombs hit," Ruby replied. "Smart dog."

The two raced for the waiting hospital trucks, threw their gear in the back and were pulled aboard by strong hands. With a roar of engines the four trucks took off. The C.O., Colonel Horan, led the convoy in the first truck.

The line of vehicles zigzagged around craters in the bomb ravaged road heading south out of the mountains towards the valley. Ruby and Bea shivered in the cold mist that engulfed the truck. The pace slowed even more as the narrow road shrouded in haze turned and twisted like a snake. Within the hour they emerged from the deep shadows of the mountains as broad sunlight beat down on the roof of the covered trucks. The temperature inside rose as did the stench of sweaty bodies. Nearing the Atomic Gold Mine the trucks screeched to a halt.

Standing in front of the lead truck, red-headed Murphy jumped up and down like a puppet on a string. One arm waved back and forth. The other he held straight out, his hand extended in a crude imitation of a traffic cop. "STOP!" he yelled. Behind Murphy was a huge crater. An unexploded bomb rested at the bottom like an egg in a nest ready to crack open at the slightest touch.

Murphy spoke to the Colonel. "Our scouts report the only road to Manila is completely impassable. In one day the Japanese have destroyed our main access to freedom. Many of our crew are already in the mountains."

The drivers jumped down from their seats and popped open the hoods of the trucks. Working rapidly they discarded spark plugs, ripped wires and hoses and smashed those engine parts they could reach.

The women jumped out to assist the troops. Working with lightning speed they ran to the back of a truck to pull down litters, and pile them with food, medical supplies and essential gear.

As a final gesture half a dozen men got behind the first two trucks and pushed, sending them careening down the mountain side, turning over and over until they burst into flames. "There's a sight to remember us by," one soldier muttered staring at the blackened hulks below.

"MOVE NOW!" a Sergeant ordered. Abandoning the other useless trucks on the road the soldiers ran at full speed to catch up with troops already in the hills. Captain Jacobs, Colonel Horan and the nurses, flanked by a half dozen troops, were right behind them.

Moving in the shadow of the mile high mountains with no easy path to follow, Ruby and Bea wasted no breath for talk. Five hours ahead was the Lusod Saw Mill where they would find food and shelter. They must keep up the pace. To slow the others down in the race to freedom would be

unforgivable. With soldiers both ahead and behind
them the women trod steadily on.

The heat and humidity rose steadily as the sun
beat down on the tree tops. Under her heavy fatigues
showers of sweat rolled down Ruby's back. Along
with the men she gagged at the heavy odor of wet
moss and frequently slipped in the slimy earth under
her feet. Most of the tangled path was little more than
a foot wide and the steeper the path the more likely it
was to slip and fall. A misstep near one of the
numerous precipices meant a certain plunge to death.

One hour passed, two hours. Before long gas
masks, tarps, pup tents and blankets fell by the
wayside. Only rifles and ammunition were kept. The
piles of discarded equipment resembled a jungle
garage sale without the buyers.

The first open area the group reached was a
small river. Colonel Horan who, from choice,
marched at the rear of the line, debated on whether to
call a halt for a brief rest when a rumble from above
shot all eyes to the sky. Out of the blazing sun came
half a dozen Japanese Zeros.

"SCATTER!" the Colonel shouted.

Within seconds Ruby, Bea and the soldiers, tripping over tangled vines, found shelter among the thick overgrowth of trees and bushes. For what seemed an eternity the messengers of death circled over the river coming in low again and again. Finally, not finding their prey the Zeros disappeared in the western sky.

The nurses and the men stayed where they were for a quarter of an hour fighting ticks and mosquitoes while waiting for a return of the enemy. At the Colonel's "All clear" the women slowly rose, stiff from their cramped position. Both stamped their legs on the sun baked river bank to restore circulation.

Ruby watched the first soldiers cross the rapidly moving river. The men held their rifles high as in some spots the water rose to their chests. Taking a deep breath Ruby followed the man in front of her. The water rose. Remaining upright took all her strength. The current was too strong. The water was too deep. She was not going to make it. She felt the river reach out for her like a hungry beast.

At that moment Ruby felt something else. Strong hands grabbed her waist, bent her in half, threw her over a shoulder and carried her across to safety. A grateful Ruby looked at her rescuer in amazement. He was just a boy probably not more than fourteen. Before she could sputter her thanks, with a wave and a grin the boy disappeared up the narrow mountain path.

"Are you okay, Ruby?" Captain Jacobs was as dripping wet as she was.

"I'm better than okay," Ruby laughed. "I'm alive!"

Despite their wet clothes Ruby and Bea pushed on. Using pure grit the women kept pace even though neither had a night's sleep since the war started. Chattering monkeys high in the trees broke the silence of the trail strongly objecting to these human invaders. Looking up, Ruby wondered at the brief flashes of light in the distance that quickly appeared and disappeared over the trees.

Gratefully sinking down at a rest stop Ruby looked up to see two mining engineers she had known in Baguio. Traveling lightly they caught up with the troops.

"Would you believe it?" one man said, "Lieutenants Bradley and Chambers! We wondered what had happened to you two. From the hills we saw Japanese soldiers swarming all over the Camp. Thought you'd been captured."

"Not yet, and don't plan to be," Ruby grinned. Despite brave smiles from both nurses the men noted their drawn faces and the dark circles under their eyes.

"Good luck," the two called passing the troops and disappearing into the hills.

"They're like mountain goats," Ruby murmured. "Sure footed and swift."

As the weary travelers put one foot in front of the other, Ruby noticed the pace slowed considerably. Almost everyone had sore feet. One young soldier with huge blisters on his feet insisted he could not go on. Ruby looked at Bea. Bea looked at Ruby and nodded. Standing on either side of the boy they lifted him up. "You CAN walk," Ruby said. "We'll help." With Bea in front and Ruby behind pushing him up the path the boy was able to put one foot in front of the other.

Another hour of silent walking and the group stopped. "Look at that!" Bea uttered. A small sure-footed donkey trotted down the hill to meet the travelers. On its back was a crudely made sign: "For The Nurses." It was a gift from the two engineers who had moved ahead.

Ruby and Bea nodded in silent agreement. They knew who would ride the donkey. The soldier with the blistered feet was so tall and his legs so long that Ruby had to tie them up. Bea got in front of the donkey and Ruby in the back. With the help of two of the soldiers along with much pulling, pushing and coaxing, the little donkey began to move.

"Captain Jacobs," a shout from the rear brought the group to a halt. "It's Colonel Horan."

The Captain ran to the end of the line to find the fallen Colonel. His face had a bluish tinge. His breathing was labored. Ruby left Bea with the donkey and ran to the Captain's side.

"Heart attack," Captain Jacobs said preparing a syringe of morphine. He turned to Ruby. "Go on ahead, take four of the men with you. I'll meet you at the Mill."

Twenty minutes later a collective sigh of relief rose from the small group as the path widened and the mill and a small house came into view. The Jorgensen family who ran the mill stood on the porch. The engineers passing by earlier told them what to expect.

Mrs. Jorgensen held out her arms to the weary nurses. "Come in, come in," she cried and led the way into a cozy combination of living room-kitchen. Yellow and blue flowered curtains covered six small windows. Beneath a vaulted ceiling the kitchen end of the room held an oversized sink complete with pump handle. A rustic bamboo table was flanked with four strong bamboo chairs. Against the opposite wall an overstuffed couch, a rare sight in the tropics, held the place of honor.

"I'll never move again," Bea sighed sinking down into its soft folds.

Mrs. Jorgensen laughed. "You will have to toss a coin as to who gets the couch as a bed tonight. Your other choice is a soft pallet on the floor."

Her words were interrupted when the door swung open. Captain Jacobs and one of the soldiers were supporting a white-faced Colonel Horan. Other troops stood guard outside. Without a word Mrs. Jorgensen led them to a back room where the Colonel was put to bed. Captain Jacobs turned to Ruby.

"He has all the signs of a heart attack. I'll leave more morphine. He needs careful monitoring for the next 48 hours. There is no way, of course that he can go on with the troops."

"Not a great Christmas gift for the Colonel," Ruby remarked realizing the next day was December 24th, Christmas Eve.

By morning the Colonel's pain eased. He was able to sit up. He insisted he could continue the trip. "No way," the doctor shook his head. "The safest place for all of you is right here." What he didn't say was that the Jorgensens, who had a telephone, learned that thousands of Japanese forces had landed just south of Manila. Manila could no longer be their destination. To continue the fight Captain Jacobs and the remaining troops would join the Filipino guerrillas in the hills.

Knowing they might not meet again the Captain forgot his rank for the moment and gave each of the nurses a hug. "The Colonel could not be in better hands," he told them as he joined the men on the steep trail.

Only a short while later a half dozen weary American troops trudged into the yard. Every one of them had sore feet. Again Ruby and Bea went into action. "Off with the boots," Ruby ordered filling buckets and pans with water to soak the feet. Soggy socks were collected and laid near the wood stove to dry.

Ruby set to work applying soothing salve to blisters while Bea brewed green tea with sugar and handed out what was left of their food. The exhausted men were speechless at finding these angels in fatigues in the middle of a jungle.

Being a long way from civilization, the Jorgensens had an ample stockpile of food. Mrs. Jorgensen prepared a Christmas feast complete with turkey and trimmings. Sitting down to such a meal that night neither Ruby nor Bea could eat. Each took small bites to please their hosts. Finally Ruby asked, "Do you mind if we take some of this food to the men out there?"

"Of course not," Mrs. Jorgensen replied.

Ruby and Bea jumped up and filled their plates, careful to take only the most plentiful foods. "Have you had enough to eat?" one soldier asked wolfing down the first real food he had tasted in three days.

"Plenty," the nurses lied in unison.

The next morning the grateful soldiers moved on but the coming days saw a steady arrival of small groups of Americans seeking safety. Some families walked for days seeking refuge from their outlying lumber camps. As a result of the trek over rough mountain trails many of the children were dehydrated with arms and legs showing insect bites and infected wounds. Ruby and Bea set up a makeshift clinic to treat the worst cases with the few medicines they had.

On December 26th a Filipino guide arrived warning that Japanese soldiers were near. Traitors with mirrors were signaling the location of American troops. These were the flashes of light Ruby had seen. There was little sleep that night. It sounded like the Japanese were all around the camp but it was only wild horses roaming the mountains.

In the morning as the sun cut through the shadows of the overgrown trees, the refugees gathered in front of the cabin. A decision that would affect them all had to be made.

# 6 SURRENDER

"If we don't waste a bite I can feed this crowd for about a week," Mrs. Jorgensen nodded looking over her dwindling food supply. The shelves would soon be bare with thirty mouths to feed. While parents would not hesitate to give their food to their children, before long even the little ones would cry with empty bellies. The same problem existed with the few medicines on hand. Morphine and antiseptics were saved for only the most serious of injuries.

Ruby, Bea and the Jorgensens gathered around Colonel Horan, who, while much improved, was still confined to bed. The Filipino guide joined the group with news. Thousands of Japanese troops had landed just east of Manila. The Japanese also held Balady Pass cutting access to the guerrilla forces higher in the mountains.

"There is no way to tell how close the Japanese are," the Colonel told the others. "To wait for undisciplined enemy soldiers to invade this camp is unthinkable. There is only one decision to be made. You will all be better off taking your chances with the Japanese in Baguio than remaining here. At least there you have a hospital."

The Jorgensens, reluctant to abandon their home, started to protest but the Colonel held up his hand. "The Japanese will loot this camp taking everything not nailed down. Don't be foolish. It can cost you your lives." He looked directly at Ruby. "I have no need of nursing. I will remain here with two of my men for a day or two then follow you down."

Ruby was well aware of what the Colonel did not say. The flashing lights seen at night meant the enemy could be on their doorstep at any moment. By remaining behind it was a sure thing Colonel Horan would be captured or killed. He refused to be carried on a litter, adding a burden to the marchers and slowing the group down.

The fierce sun overhead signaled midday, not the best time to begin such a demanding march. A noon departure meant the real possibility of spending a night on the trail but waiting until morning was not an option. Ruby spoke to the families telling them of the Colonel's decision. "Carry as little as possible," she told each family. "Bring water, any food you have and warm clothing for a night on the trail. The enemy could be here at any time. We cannot wait until tomorrow to make the trip."

The lumber camp looked like someone had stuck a stick in a beehive. Families scattered in all directions, gathering sweaters and jackets, filling canteens with water while soothing crying children who quickly picked up on the anxiety of their worried parents. Husbands pleaded with wives to leave behind treasured keepsakes. A Dresden figurine would be of no use in a Japanese internment camp. The disorganized became organized as within minutes the Americans were ready to leave.

Under a blazing sun a somber line of men, women and children began the long walk down the narrow logging path. The guide and three Filipino solders led while three others took up the rear, guns ready for any attack by the enemy. Within an hour the blue sky vanished. Clouds drifted up from the south. The day turned humid and hot. There was little talking. All energy was directed to placing one foot in front of the other with eyes glued to the slippery twisting trail. Ears were tuned to every slapping branch or snapping twig, which could mean danger. Ruby and Bea took turns relieving exhausted mothers of the youngest children who had to be carried.

The families moved at a turtle's pace. The winding mountain trail was treacherous with uneven spots. Thick roots reached out for unsuspecting feet. Many of the children slipped and fell forcing frequent halts. Ruby and Bea handed the babies to their mothers to check for injuries. With each inspection Ruby breathed a sigh of relief. There was only a scraped elbow or knee, no broken bones. The slow progress however meant there was no way they could reach Baguio by nightfall.

As dusk clipped the top of the trees the guide called a halt. A small clearing edged with lauan (tall grass) and shadowed by mahogany trees and tall pines would do for the night. One family gathered piles of leaves to serve as beds. Mothers stretched aching arms as they laid their children down. Meager food supplies were pooled and the families dined on tinned beef, tuna and cold baked beans. Smiles were seen for the first time that day when Bea brought out the box of candy for dessert.

Ruby and Bea went from group to group to warn parents to check themselves and their children for ticks. Those who brought jackets and sweaters were grateful for their warmth. Few had blankets for protection against the chilly night air ever present during the dry season. Children slept cuddled close to their parents.

Filipino soldiers at each end of the clearing stood watch over the makeshift camp as the weary travelers settled for the night. A baby's cry or the murmuring of a child soon gave way to the night sounds of a wakeful mountain.

The guide assured the group there was no danger from cloud rats emerging at night from hollow trees or the hundreds of bats catching insects on the fly overhead. These sounds were not nearly as disturbing to a wide-awake Ruby as the constant whine of mosquitoes.

She sat a bit apart from the group her back resting against a large pine. The thought that kept her awake was the treacherous river that had to be crossed. The children could be carried on the backs of the men, but what about the women and the elderly? One misstep and the river would reach out like a giant hand, grasp them and toss them downstream to ride the current as easily as a paper boat on an ocean wave. There was no way several of the group could survive the crossing without help.

Ruby dozed off and on through the night and opened her eyes to a morning sun that cut through the gray haze of the mountain. As she stood, her stiff neck, arms and legs protested. Bending and stretching helped. She ran her tongue over her teeth. How she missed such a simple thing as a toothbrush. She shook twigs and leaves out of her hair and started her rounds of the families. Sleepy children awoke and wandered into the bushes to relieve themselves under the watchful eye of a parent. The group again shared its meager food supplies. Two of the men built a small fire and cheers went up as one woman produced a tin of coffee. No one worried about the noise. If the Japanese were that close, capture was inevitable. If not, they would make it to their destination.

The previous day's march left the Americans with little energy. None was wasted in talking. Women gathered up clothing used as pillows on the hard ground. It was then a scream shattered the quiet camp. "My baby! My baby!"

The mother was frantic. Only the day before she herded four children down the path with no mishaps. Finally her companions understood. Her two-year-old had wandered off. Mothers gathered their children closer to them as the men fanned out to begin the search. Precious minutes flew by. The only sound was the snapping of twigs under tramping feet as the search area widened. A shout echoed through the mountain.

"HERE!" A triumphant Mr. Jorgensen stepped out from the trees carrying a little boy who had chased a butterfly into the trees. The mother grabbed her child hugging him with tears of joy while at the same time scolding him for running off.

The search for the missing boy delayed the group nearly half an hour. The marchers gathered the last of their belongings and with hesitant strides resumed the last leg of the journey leading them to an uncertain future.

The walk down the mountain was easier when lower levels were reached. At the same time Ruby's concern about the river grew. In the distance she heard the ripple of water wearing away unsuspecting rocks. Rounding a twist in the trail they stepped on to the rock-strewn shore she remembered so well. The waters had risen since the last crossing. The current ran as strong as ever. What would happen now? Watching the rolling river some of the mothers wondered the same thing.

"Follow me," the guide instructed turning west and leading the group past the dangerous crossing.

Ruby's great sigh of relief could be heard all the way to the front of the line when they rounded a sharp bend in the path revealing a narrow, shallow river crossing. The ripple of water here was so low they could barely get their feet wet. Delighted children waded and splashed and begged their parents to let them cross again and again.

The silence deepened as the group trudged on. Even the children were quiet sensing the unspoken fears of their parents. One hour passed, two. Hats came off long enough to wipe sweat that ran down the brow into the eyes, then quickly put back on as protection from the blazing sun. With no new mishaps the pace was steady.

"Look," Bea called out. From their mountain perch the travelers spotted the headquarters building of Camp John Hay. They watched soldiers moving back and forth on the parade ground like tiny worker ants. The large Japanese flag laid out on the ground was gone. Unknown to the travelers many of the recently released Japanese internees put on uniforms and joined the soldiers. In the distance they saw the tops of buildings in Baguio. Many appeared to have been spared by the bombs.

"We leave you here. God go with you," the guide said as he and the remaining Filipinos disappeared quickly as if swallowed up by the mountain. No guide was needed for the end of the journey. Ruby hoped the soldiers would check on Colonel Horan as the men continued up the mountain to find some way to join the fight for freedom.

Like a tiny, slow-moving avalanche, a tired and scraggly group of Americans rolled out of the mountain late in the morning of December 28th. The smell of charred wood lingered in the air as smoke rose from burned out barracks. The hospital Ruby noted with relief had not been touched. Two of Ruby's favorite corpsmen waved from the hospital steps. The Americans stepped on to a dirt road pock-marked with craters large and small. Here and there an unexploded bomb lay by the roadside, a souvenir left by the Japanese bombers.

Most menacing, however, was the sight of their welcome party. Stone-faced Japanese soldiers stood before them in a solid line, rifles ready, bayonets fixed.

"They are going to murder us all," one woman murmured. "Hush!" her husband warned.

Behind the soldiers were two ten-ton Army trucks with engines running. Those standing near could feel the heat from the exhaust. At a quick command, two soldiers ran forward, loosened the chains and lowered the gates. All that was needed was passengers. Motioning with his gun a Captain motioned to the captives to climb into the trucks. A mother who needed help handed her baby to Ruby. Within seconds the hard steel blade of a bayonet was thrust across Ruby's chest, preventing her from stepping forward and handing the baby back.

"My baby," the mother screamed. Hands reached out to stop her from climbing out of the truck.

Ruby pointed to the baby and then to herself and shook her head NO. A second time she pointed to the baby and then to the hysterical mother and nodded

YES. The soldier grinned with yellow-stained teeth and lowered his rifle. Ignoring the soldier Ruby lifted the baby up to the grateful mother. *The Japanese like to play games*, Ruby thought in disgust.

Last to climb aboard Ruby and Bea found the jam-packed truck allowed for standing room only. The covered tarp gave no protection from the heat, which mixed with the smell of unwashed, sweat-soaked bodies made breathing difficult. The open sides meant that dust from the road would add to the misery. In quiet undertones there was murmuring among the captives about their destination. Would they be taken to Baguio and released? It seemed highly unlikely. Had the Japanese set up an internment camp for all Americans? If so, where? Or were they to be taken to a remote area to be killed by rifles or machine guns? Speculation grew as the trucks continued to idle.

A Japanese Major approached the truck and peered in with cold darting eyes. Despite his short stature he stood as straight as if a poker were up his back. There was not a speck of dust on his tailored uniform. Across his chest were numerous medals. He was not a young man. His stomach revealed the slight bulge of middle age. He carried a swagger stick similar to those carried by British officers. Ruby got the impression of a rascal, intelligent and shrewd.

He pointed to Ruby and Bea who were surprised that he spoke English. "You are Army nurses?" he asked. Ruby nodded. He had evidently seen their greeting by the hospital corpsmen. He studied the two women. "Most unusual," he said. "Women in the Army? It is unheard of, a barbaric custom. There are no women in the Japanese army. You two get off," he ordered.

"They are going to shoot us, that's what they're going to do, they're going to shoot us," Bea cried. She looked again at the row of bayonets. "Our heads are going to come off."

Ruby gave Bea a nudge in the ribs. "Well, wait until they do it," she said.

To the nurses' surprise they followed the Major to an Army sedan. Japanese flags were mounted on the front. The Major pointed to the back seat. Ruby and Bea climbed in accompanied by a guard. The driver and the English-speaking officer sat in front. The officer turned and spoke to the women. "I am Major Mukibo," he said. "Do not be concerned. You will not be harmed."

As the sedan turned toward Baguio the Major fired questions about the town and Camp John Hay. As Army nurses the only questions they were allowed to answer were name, rank and serial number. When the questions stopped neither nurse said a word as the sedan weaving around potholes and craters covered the short distance to Baguio. There, Ruby was amazed to see the Filipino citizens going about their business. Next to a bombed out restaurant was a busy shoe shop. More collapsed buildings were followed by more shops some with cardboard where windows had been. Ruby did notice that any citizen who passed a Japanese soldier stopped and bowed. The bow was always returned.

The sedan pulled to a stop in front of the President's summer palace. The Major marveled at the elegantly designed main building, an architectural jewel poised at the head of lush green grounds. "This will serve as the headquarters of the Japanese Imperial Army," he stated. "Most appropriate."

Bea leaned over to whisper in Ruby's ear. "I didn't know what to expect, but it sure wasn't a sightseeing tour." Ruby smiled and squeezed Bea's hand.

The tour ended abruptly at Brent School. To the nurses' great surprise, the Major got out and shook their hands. "You will care for the people," he said. With no further word he entered the sedan that quickly disappeared in the distance.

"Care for who and with what?" Ruby wondered as they entered the building flanked by two soldiers. She soon found out. Five hundred American civilian prisoners including those from the march down the mountain were crowded into space designed for two hundred fifty. None of the upstairs rooms were used. The internees were confined in jam-packed rooms on the first floor. Once again the smell of sweat-soaked, unwashed bodies was nearly overwhelming. Despite being surrounded by misery, Ruby couldn't help smiling. This room must have been the kindergarten.

The walls were lined with children's drawings of familiar animals. There were smiling crocodiles, monkeys, snakes, toucans and tarsiers (small animals with owl-like eyes).

Many of the captives had stories to tell. "Late last night Japanese soldiers banged on the doors of our homes. If a door didn't open fast enough they smashed it in with the butts of their rifles. Then we were ordered out," one woman told the nurses. "We had little time to bring anything with us. They forced us to walk to this school and to stand in a crowded room for three hours until they finally allowed us to sleep on the floor. Soldiers manned machine guns at every exit. They just sat there staring at us not moving a muscle but looking as if they would take pleasure in killing us all. The constant tramp of heavy boots around the building went on all night and kept most of us awake. This morning they let a few move to other rooms. At noon they brought us watery soup. Everyone is hungry."

Ruby and Bea set off to visit the other prisoners and, at the same time, get a better look at the layout of the first floor. There was no question of escape.

"Eureka!" Bea cried as she looked through an open door at the kitchen. She ran to the sink and tried the taps. A huge grin spread across her face as water gushed out. The prisoners could survive longer without food than without water.

With Ruby as a lookout Bea explored drawers and cabinets finding the soldiers had taken anything useful, knives, can openers, pots, pans and dishes. "Look what they missed," she whispered opening the door to a cold oven. "Someone has left a ham. What a treasure!" Bea quickly snatched it up and put it under her shirt.

Shouting orders no one understood, the Japanese soldiers, using their guns, roughly weeded out the men prisoners herding them to a dirt road some distance away. Then to the horror of their mothers, crying children were pulled from their arms and taken away along with several older women. Pleading was useless. Mothers who clung to their children were roughly knocked aside. One woman, still pleading, rose with blood running down her face. Ruby was helpless. Soldiers stood in her way as she tried to get to the woman to stop the bleeding. The women watched in horror as the children were carried fighting and screaming to the tennis courts.

It was then the reason for the separations became clear. The isolated groups of men and women turned to face a row of manned machine guns.

"They're going to get us all," Bea murmured still hiding the ham but by now resigned to their fate. Several minutes passed. There was some discussion among the lower ranking officers. Angry voices were raised. Ruby wondered if they were arguing about who would dispose of the bodies. The shouting came to an abrupt halt when the Major's car which had evidently turned around, entered the compound. The driver hopped out and ran around to open a rear door. Major Mukibo stepped out. This time he ignored the prisoners and approached the officers.

Minutes crept by as the Americans and Japanese soldiers silently stared at each other across the loaded machine guns. Highly disciplined, no soldier dared move a muscle even to reach up to wipe sweat away. Meanwhile the Major appeared to be berating the other officers. Eventually the Captain in charge bowed to the Major.

Major Mukibo's orders would be carried out. Without appearing to move, Ruby slid her foot over to touch Bea's shoe with her own nodding when she heard the word "hostages."

The prisoners who also heard the word let out a collective sigh of relief. They watched with silent cheers when the soldiers lifted the machine guns and put them on trucks. The English-speaking Major turned to the captives. "You will return to the building. Your children will be brought to you. You must tell us where all guns and weapons are hidden in your homes so that these can be collected. If you do as you are told the Japanese soldiers will treat you with kindness."

While relieved families were reunited, it was again a restless night at Brent School. The captives were given watery soup with tiny bits of meat, not nearly enough to delay hunger. The silence of the long night was broken by cries of hungry children.

Few adults slept. The late December air in Baguio was cold and few had warm clothing or blankets.

December 29th brought another long day of waiting. It was four o'clock in the afternoon when dozens of soldiers marched into the school. Ruby looked around for the Major. He was nowhere to be seen.

One soldier who spoke broken English gave the orders. "You move to new place. Take only what you can carry." There was a restless stirring among the Americans many of whom had dozed off, exhausted from the previous sleepless night. Guns shoved in their backs awakened sleepers. It was a hungry group of captives who gathered their belongings for the two mile walk to Scout Hill. The Japanese ordered Filipino citizens to watch the defeated Americans, who rather than being humiliated, walked with heads held high.

Beatrice and Ruby had hardly anything to carry. They had given everything away except one blanket. Ruby carried one of the children a short distance. Some people had small babies, perhaps two or three of them. Others had big bags of things. The march ended in front of an old barracks, the roof pock-marked with shrapnel holes. It was the same barracks that had briefly housed the Japanese internees before the soldiers arrived and set them free.

Ruby stared at the dilapidated building in dismay. How could a building intended to house fifty or sixty men possible hold 500 internees? A low moan ran through the crowd. Most were thinking the same thing. Was there a kitchen? Was there running water? How about toilet facilities? Where would they sleep? The Japanese guards surrounded the crowd, rifles ready. Children, too exhausted to cry, clung to their mothers. The prisoners would soon have answers to their questions.

In front of the barracks was a crudely made sign: IGOROT BARRACKS. Peeling paint, windows without screens and broken boards on the outside told the story of what the prisoners found on the inside. As the captives entered the barracks nauseating odors pinched their nostrils. The Japanese internees previously housed in the barracks had tossed garbage everywhere and did not use toilets. There were bare rafters. Nails jutting out of the walls would soon be used for hanging clothes and ropes dangling from rafters would serve as clothes lines. There were no lights, no water, no food and no toilets. As far as the exhausted Americans knew, this was to be their home until the end of the war... if they survived.

# 7 PRISONER

The stunned Americans stood shoulder to shoulder in the midst of filth and decay. Dirt mixed with dust from the bombings covered every inch of the floors. Rats' nests nestled in piles of garbage. Windows and doors with no screens invited swarms of flies

As Ruby stood surrounded by the captives she realized that they would be fighting an enemy far more deadly than the Japanese army. The filthy, overcrowded barracks was a breeding ground for disease, particularly dysentery. Yet two well-dressed women standing near Ruby showed little concern for their fate. One chattered away to a friend while applying makeup. "I'm sure," she said, "My servants will arrive shortly to do whatever cleaning is needed."

Ruby shook her head. Those who came from wealthy homes with many servants were in for a shock. At first they refused to accept the sudden and drastic changes in their lives. Reality would soon set in.

One reality was that some sort of order was needed to make living conditions bearable. Ruby wasn't worried. Americans are great at organizing and she was sure that leaders would soon step forward. She was right. One miner climbed on a box yelling for quiet.

"We'll have to use our heads to survive. Cleaning means water. The closest water is a mile away. You men, grab all the buckets you can find while I talk to the guards. In the meantime, Murphy, see what you can do with that." He pointed to water pipes destroyed by earlier bombings.

"Will do," Murphy called out and Ruby recognized the cheerful Irishman who had dug the air raid shelter for the hospital. Was it only two weeks ago? It seemed like two years with all that had happened.

"Look over there," Bea pointed to a small group near the door. Ruby and Bea made their way to two civilian doctors, Dr. Nance and Dr. Haugwout and several missionary nurses.

"Ruby, Beatrice!" Dr. Nance gave both nurses a hug. "Welcome to the barracks medical team with nothing to treat patients with but a smile."

"One thing I can do," Dr. Haugwout added, "is to give a series of talks to impress on everyone the absolute necessity for keeping clean. Water must be boiled. Hands washed frequently even if there is no soap. Floors washed daily, soiled clothing washed and boiled and laid out in the sun for at least two hours. Our greatest enemy is disease and this is the only way to fight it."

"We'll go from group to group and collect any medicines that might be of use," Ruby added. "We can set up a small table to act as a dispensary during the day." She looked around at the mass of people and the small amount of floor space. "Bea and I can sleep under the table at night."

Within an hour the bucket brigade brought enough water for a first cleaning. Despite those few waiting for servants who would never appear, there were more than enough willing hands to sweep out the garbage and wipe down the floors. Older children were assigned to a fly swatting detail. One prisoner donated a candy bar for the child who killed the most flies. At the same time more engineers from the mines found the best spot for outside latrines and the men dug in relays to complete them that same night.

"LOOK!" Ruby couldn't tell where the shout came from. The guards opened the gates to allow two trucks to enter. Were they bringing more prisoners? In this hugely overcrowded barracks where would they put more people?

Riding in the first truck was a German, Mr. Spatz, who brought two mattresses and promised more. Civilians from Baguio jumped down from the second truck and unloaded case after case of canned goods and water. Under Dr. Haugwout's watchful eye food was heated. Hungry prisoners had their first real meal in twenty-four hours.

There was little sleep for the prisoners that night. The few mattresses and mats were given to the children and the older people. Some of the Americans from Baguio brought a few possessions with them but had no place to put them. They used their bundles for pillows. With only inches between and no room to turn over, most laid awake on the hard floor without blankets shivering in the cold mountain air.

At dawn the tramp of heavy boots along with rifles in their faces got the weary prisoners to their feet. Men, women and children were marched outside and made to stand and watch as the American flag was taken down, trampled on and torn up. There were many silent tears as the Japanese flag, the rising sun, flew from the same flagpole.

As the days passed little by little order emerged from chaos. A committee was elected to determine work details. Weeks that followed were spent cleaning up and fixing up. One mother gathered the children together for songs in the evening. With no bedtime stories to read other mothers took turns telling stories recalling those tales of princesses and knights they had learned as children.

At night mattresses were edge to edge and getting up was impossible without stumbling over someone. The same mattresses were rolled up during the day to allow space to move around. Each captive was given a number and required to line up every morning on the tennis courts for roll call and the hated flag raising.

Food, mostly rice with a few vegetables, was delivered daily and teams of cooks worked in crude kitchens to provide two meals a day. With more than 500 people to feed garbage piled up. Men vied for a place on the garbage detail since it allowed them to leave the camp for a short time. Weeks on meager rations meant that two or three men had to carry a single garbage container to a spot where a pit was dug and waste was buried. In their spare time the weary and weakened men built a wagon to haul the containers. They built it so that it would take more people to work it so more men could get off the grounds.

For those on the wood gathering detail it meant a chance to bring back priceless soap hidden in the woods by the departing army. No one tried to escape. The Japanese made it clear that for each person who attempted to escape ten would be shot.

Despite all the cleaning efforts dysentery broke out during the night of January 2nd. Ruby and Dr. Nance climbed over numerous sleepers to attend to three desperately ill children. There was little they could do for them. "Hand washing could have prevented this, Why won't people listen?" Dr. Nance moaned.

On January 4th the Commandant of the camp, Col. Nakamura, ordered the men moved to another barracks. While this helped to relieve the crowding, husbands and wives were allowed only brief visits in the evening on the tennis courts. The doctors were permitted a brief time each morning to visit the women's barracks to care for the ill.

As day after dreary day passed with its never-ending battle for cleanliness, tempers flared. Shirkers found ways to cause work for others. Fights broke out when one mattress took up more than its share of space. Every captive jealously guarded what she considered to be her exclusive territory.

Then came the night the nurses faced their biggest challenge. Thirteen women in the barracks were expecting babies. The Commanding General of the Japanese Army was given a list of their names and due dates. It was agreed that they could go to the civilian hospital in Baguio for the births.

"RUBY, COME!" The yell came from women standing around a mattress in the center of the room. It was 10:00 p.m. on January 30th. Isabelle Scott was in labor. A quick check told Ruby that she must be taken to the hospital at once. Ruby sent word by the guards to bring a car to the front of the barracks and to send for one of the doctors. When the apologetic guards returned they told Ruby, "Honorable General say doctor not needed. Woman must wait until Monday morning to go to hospital."

Ruby looked the guard in the eye. "Well, this is Saturday night and babies don't wait like that!"

The guard mumbled, "General is a great General but he does not know anything about babies."

"Then send for one of the doctors," Ruby pleaded.

The guard shook his head. "Men not allowed in barracks at night."

Ruby knew that arguing was of no use. "Let's go," she told Bea. The two moved the woman to a small storeroom and placed her on a thin mattress on the floor.

The eight by ten foot storeroom was barely large enough for the mattress let alone the nurses. Outside the small room confusion reigned as soldiers entered the barracks ordering the missionary captives to gather their belongings. Sleepy children howled as their mothers dressed them for the trip. They were told that they would be taken to a hotel in Baguio where they would be processed and set free. Mumbling among themselves most were skeptical that freedom was that easy. The other captives were grateful for the additional space when the mothers and children were led away.

"We need light," Ruby yelled. The barracks had electricity by this time but the storeroom had one small 40 watt bulb hanging by a frayed wire from the ceiling. A sympathetic guard brought lanterns. The next problem was where to put them. There was barely room to turn around. Ruby solved the problem by hanging them on nails sticking out of the walls.

Outside the storeroom the prisoners heard the soft cries of a woman in pain. Ruby opened a can of ether and used a tea strainer with cotton inside as a mask. Fortunately, the Irishman Murphy had restored the water pipes. Bea boiled their few instruments in a fire bucket over a wood fire. Eleven o'clock passed. Midnight. One a.m. The woman's cries were fainter. "Soon, now," Ruby's soft voice reassured the mother.

At one thirty in the morning a baby's lusty cry echoed throughout the barracks. "I'd cry, too, being born in a place like this," Ruby smiled at the little one.

"About seven pounds and all's well," a relieved Ruby told the waiting women.

Word quickly spread to the men's barracks. They knew that everything was all right with the birth. All agreed the first baby born in Igorot Barracks should be named John Hay Scott. While the mother disagreed and named her son Richard Hawkins, the first name stuck while the mother and child were in the camp. One of the women, Natalie Crouter, said, "We went in to see Isobel and celebrated with peppermint sticks while watching the baby learn to drink."

Territorial fights were forgotten as joyful women throughout the barracks made a crib from a box and lined it with part of a blanket. Unrolled gauze became a mosquito net. An old towel turned into two diapers. A tiny shirt was fashioned from a flannel nightgown. "Not the latest fashion in layettes," one woman remarked. "But it will have to do." The tired but grateful mother had tears in her eyes as she accepted the women's offerings. "How kind," she murmured. "How very kind."

The Japanese guards were also delighted. "Is more needed?" the guard with the broken English asked Ruby.

"A heater would be nice," Ruby said never expecting to see one. Imagine her surprise when the guard returned with a heater taken from his own barracks. The arrival of the first baby at Camp John Hay was a big event for everyone! Little was Ruby to guess that within the next three months at that same camp she would assist in the births of thirteen babies, eleven American, one English and one Chinese. Not just the nurses, but all imprisoned in Igorot Barracks no longer believed their stay there would be a short one.

As days turned into weeks, cases of dysentery were on the rise. Unfortunately there were still many in the barracks who did not take seriously the need for constant washing of themselves and their bedding and clothing. The desperately ill needed to be separated from the rest but there was no place to put them.

In mid February six weeks after the internment of the Americans the Japanese gave permission to establish a hospital. But as with all permissions rules were attached. The hospital was to be used exclusively for dysentery cases. In Ruby's words:

*The building authorized was a small cottage that had been the home of an officer. The living room was used as a ward for women and children. One bedroom was a nursery and one bedroom was used for adult male patients. The laundry room was painted and used as an operating room and a delivery room. An operating table was constructed from old pieces of lumber and padded with a blanket. There were usually more patients than beds so the less acutely ill were treated in the barracks and the severe cases were treated in the hospital.*

Ruby and Bea were kept busy boiling all bed linen and clothing used by patients and exposing it to sunshine for two hours. When soap became practically non-existent, soap was made from lye obtained from wood ashes then mixed with fats and oils. It worked but it was very hard on the hands.

Fortunately the Japanese paid no attention to the laundry room and the operating table since they had decreed that no operations would be performed. Either they had no idea of the purpose of the room or they decided to ignore it.

"Working without instruments or supplies is the same as having no hands," Dr. Nance complained to Ruby. "If I can talk Nakamura into it would you go down to the Army hospital with us?"

"Tell him we need toilet paper," Ruby suggested. "I'll be glad to go. I know where things are."

Nakamura sent word that Dr. Nance, Dr. Walker, a dentist, and Ruby could make the trip to the Army hospital to bring back toilet paper and nothing else. No medicines or surgical instruments were to be touched. These were saved for Japanese soldiers fighting for the glory of the Emperor and the Imperial Japanese Army.

The four captives sat on the floor of an old 1936 Ford truck that hit every bump in the road. Ruby worried that if she did find the surgical instruments she had hidden they would be difficult to conceal on the return trip.

"Don't worry about what we need or don't need. We need everything," Dr. Nance said. "Smuggle out whatever you can. Hide the supplies under the toilet paper."

The rickety truck ground to a halt in front of the hospital. Ruby was astonished at the changes she saw. In just one short month the pristine white building was covered with splotches of dirt and mud. The roof was pock-marked with shrapnel. The entrance door hung crazily to the side by one hinge. Screens were ripped away. Steps revealed deep cracks from the stomping of heavy boots. The empty rooms meant that soldiers in the Japanese Imperial Army must be cared for in the fully staffed and supplied civilian hospitals in Baguio.

*If this is the outside,* Ruby thought, *What will we find inside?*

The four entered a once cheerful entrance hall now drab and uninviting with dust and dirt everywhere. The bare admissions desk spoke of Japanese soldiers who had helped themselves to scissors, staplers, pens, pencils, flashlights and anything else that was not part of the fixtures. A speaker above the desk hung by a single wire like a macabre wall decoration.

"Follow me," Ruby said, leading the way to a storeroom where cartons of toilet paper were stacked ceiling high.

"We'll hide what we can in the toilet paper cartons before we take them to the truck but we'll have to work fast," Dr. Nance replied.

As if chased by tigers the four could not have moved faster. Pointing the doctors in the direction of the surgery, Ruby headed for the supply room surprised the Japanese looters had missed small amounts of powdered morphine, aspirin and four precious bars of soap. She tucked them in her pocket. "Darn," she mumbled to herself. There were no antiseptics for wounds. Wasting no more time in the nearly empty room Ruby sought out the corner where she had hidden surgical instruments before her escape up the mountain.

There! To her surprise, the instruments she had wrapped so carefully over a month before were still resting behind the big box. There were bone instruments, surgical scissors, retractors, hemostats and forceps. She was relieved that the instruments were wrapped so that they made no noise. Working as fast as she could Ruby tucked them under her clothing and stuffed them in her waistband. She stopped when she heard the heavy clump of boots. She looked up in dismay to see a guard watching her from the doorway. Had he seen her hide the instruments? Short and stocky with a scar running down one cheek he leaned against the door staring at her. She heard the soldiers were not eating any better than the prisoners but this guard looked healthy enough. He took a step forward making guttural sounds in Japanese that she did not understand.

A shout from the hallway caught the guard's attention. "Enough time, all leave now." The guard watching Ruby motioned with his rifle.

Ruby hid her trembling hands and gave a sigh of relief as she meekly followed the guard outside.

The doctors took their time strolling back and forth to the truck loading boxes of toilet paper. The Ford was so overloaded that the doctors and one guard stood on the running board while the driver motioned for Ruby to sit up front with him. The weight of the concealed instruments was such that Dr. Nance grabbed Ruby's rear and gave her a shove as she attempted to climb up without dropping anything. The return trip over the bumpy road had the doctors holding their breaths. If a box should fall the supplies they gathered would spill into the road with the toilet paper.

The minute the truck pulled up in front of the hospital Ruby jumped out, took the steps two at a time and ran as fast as she could to hide the instruments under the mattress of one of the patients.

"Latrine," Dr. Nance said shaking his head and pointing to the disappearing Ruby. The guard nodded as if he understood.

As soon as Ruby returned the guard announced, "Everyone must be searched." Ruby and the doctors turned out their pockets with nothing in them. Fortunately the guard did not think to check the boxes of toilet paper.

Three days after the hospital opened, the first operation, an appendectomy, was performed. Ruby and Bea scrubbed the operating room top to bottom with Lysol solution. Sterilizing was a challenge. The water from rusty pipes was filled with sediment and could not be used to boil instruments. Ruby decided to put the instruments on a tray and bake them in the oven of a wood-burning cook stove for twenty minutes at 400 degrees. The patient was given drop ether as an anesthetic and to the delight of the medical team, came through with no infection. For whatever reason the guards pretended they didn't know what was going on.  Since surgical supplies could not be replaced, the nurses found ways to use them again and again. They washed sponges and drapes in cold water, laying them on a wire net to dry in the sunshine for two hours. They washed dressings and dried them in the oven of the wood-burning cook stove. While these tasks were time consuming, Ruby took pride in the fact that there were no infections following surgeries.

Days became weeks and weeks became months. By now those who thought the war would end quickly knew better. The little news leaking into the camp told of the fierce fighting of American troops in Europe. All of the war effort was going in that direction. Once Hitler was defeated attention would be given to the South Pacific. Winning back the Philippines was not high on President Roosevelt's priority list. Surprisingly the Japanese treated the nurses and doctors in the small hospital with respect. Even so, it was puzzling when Commandant Nakamura sent for Dr. Nance.

"You must prepare to move your hospital to a new camp," he said. "I give you this warning so that nothing is left behind. You must say nothing to others."

Ignoring the warning not to talk of the move Dr. Nance told Ruby and Bea to start packing. Surgeries were cancelled. Nakamura would allow critically ill patients to be taken to the hospital in Baguio. All others were returned to their barracks to be treated as clinic patients.

"Well," Ruby mused, "Wherever we're going it couldn't be worse so it has to be better."

# 8 A SURPRISE MOVE

Rumors flew inside the camp like angry wasps. Get ready to move! Where? No one knew for sure but one thing they did know, the Japanese were up to something. On April 22nd the cooks watched for food trucks that did not arrive. They made do with leftovers from the day before which were practically nothing considering they were feeding hundreds of people twice a day. They could not raid the garden since Nakamura ordered garden workers to pick all the vegetables and load them on trucks for transport.

On April 23rd guards rolled back the chicken wire to admit five six-wheel trucks. Mud splattered and with missing doors, the ancient Fords jerked to a stop at the edge of the parade ground. Even from a distance those watching smelled the rank odor of oil spills on the wooden decks. The sagging canvas tops pockmarked with shrapnel gave little protection from the fierce sun. Threadbare tires and cracked windshields hinted at the trucks' age. These trucks, which had once carried elite troops, were now, before ending on a scrap heap, delegated to hauling prisoners.

The women's barracks were a mixture of bedlam and chaos. Afraid of what they would find at their new destination, mothers ran frantically back and forth from clotheslines to mattresses stuffing bags with rags that served as diapers, rice bowls made from half a coconut, tattered clothing...all priceless possessions. Sensing the anxiety of their mothers, babies howled. Questions from anxious older children were endless.

"NO TIME!" a guard yelled at one middle-aged mother notorious for spoiling her two teen-aged daughters by doing their work. She was helping them pack make-up and nail polish in a gilt edged cosmetic box. "NO TIME!" he yelled again. With a sweep of his rifle the guard knocked the box to the floor filling the air with the scent of a broken bottle of Tabu perfume. Tangee lipsticks and a rainbow of nail polishes scattered across the floor. With the butt of his rifle he pushed the girls aside as they scrambled to pick up their treasures.

"MOVE! MOVE." More stone-faced guards stomped on bags, boxes and clothing determined to carry out their orders and empty the barracks as rapidly as possible.

At the hospital Ruby, Bea and Doctor Nance moved at top speed collecting all the things they could not pack in advance. Like an assembly line medicines, surgical instruments and partially dried dressings passed from Dr. Nance to Ruby to Bea to fill overstuffed duffel bags. A guard stood in the door pointing to the parade ground with his rifle. "MOVE! MOVE!" he yelled.

"Must be the only word of English he knows," Ruby muttered.

"Wait," Bea called. She disappeared down the hallway heading for the empty women's ward. Making a beeline for a small cabinet she dropped to her knees and removed a key from a chain around her neck. She grinned from ear to ear as she unlocked the cabinet and reached back to pull out her most priceless possession, an unopened tin of corned beef.

Dr. Nance looked puzzled.

"That can of corned beef goes wherever she goes," Ruby explained. "She got it from a Red Cross package and is never without it. Off duty she gets it out, handles it and touches it but never opens it. When I asked her why, she said she didn't dare open it because that would be the end of everything."

Dr. Nance nodded. "It's more than a can of corned beef," he observed. "It's a can of hope."

Outside the trucks' engines idled while lines of prisoners shuffled across the dusty parade ground toward the ancient Fords. Many women carried a baby in one arm while dragging a bag with their few possessions behind. Toddlers clung to their mother's skirts. Guards stopped the few from the men's barracks who drug mattresses behind them. "NO ROOM," they yelled pointing to the trucks. Protesting was useless. Arguing with a bayonet is not wise. Even so the men looked back with considerable regret to see their mattresses left in the parade ground dust.

The five trucks could hold a tenth of the prisoners so many trips to the new camp were necessary. Women and children were loaded first with cramped standing room only.

The trucks sputtered and choked their way along the Bontoc Trail high in the mountains on the other side of Baguio. Their destination was Camp John Holmes. The women were so tightly packed that even when the trucks took a sharp curve they could not fall. Little did the Americans know that the Japanese used Camp Holmes as a buffer between the guerrilla forces to the north and Baguio to the south. If any shooting started the guerrillas would shoot into the camp and the Japanese would shoot over the prisoners and get the guerrillas.

The medical team was among the first to step down from the rickety, jolting trucks. The camp, larger than Camp John Hay, was surrounded by chicken wire mixed with barbed wire. "Things are looking up," Ruby mumbled taking in three fairly new barracks built for Filipino troops before the bombing. Two were two stories high. Men, when they arrived, were assigned to the one level barracks. Women and children made their way to the others. They found double deck bunk beds upstairs. The beds were wooden with planks and no mattresses. Ruby was glad to see shell paned windows to keep the flies out. She was not happy to find bedbugs crawling all over the bunks.

On the lower floors were the kitchen and mess hall as well as several smaller rooms. The kitchen housed two huge cauldrons hanging above a concrete oven. The prisoner cooks from Camp John Hay would have to learn a new way of cooking.

The large parade ground boasted a guard house, administration building, a small hospital with a separate annex for babies, and a shop building where engineers and miners would attempt to make anything necessary to daily life.

In the shop it wasn't long before American ingenuity outdid itself. From a small piece of aluminum a businessman and a dentist made a pair of false teeth. One young lady had a tooth replaced on her bridge with a carved piece of bone. A beautiful cup was pounded from a brass doorknob. Corn grinders, peanut shellers and banana sorters were turned out. Washboards were fashioned from bamboo. The blacksmith made a knife, a hammer, an axe and two frying pans. Wooden shoes were worn by practically all of the internees. Measurements were taken with a small piece of cloth and a strap was attached.

One of the things missing in the move was the garbage wagon. While every scrap of food was used, with more than 400 people there was garbage to be disposed of. The men, weakened from a steady diet of rice were unable to hand carry the heavy garbage pails more than a mile to the open pit. They had to have their garbage wagon.

A small delegation approached the administration building with a request to see Nakamura. The request was granted. Nakamura nodded his agreement and eight men set out to walk back down the winding trail to retrieve the wagon.

Arriving at Camp John Hay the men were relieved to see the contraption right where they left it. They took turns pulling the cumbersome wagon on foot to Camp Holmes with a Japanese guard riding on top.

Just as they had when arriving at Camp John Hay, the first priority for the Americans was getting water running into the barracks and scrubbing down the floors with Lysol. Since work crews were assigned at Camp John Hay the same crews went to work at Camp John Holmes.

At the hospital Ruby and Bea were washing down the treatment rooms and counting supplies when visitors arrived. Five very plainly dressed women stood in the doorway.

"We're not open for business yet," Ruby called out. "We came to help," one of the women replied. "We're nurses." The women quickly told their story. They were among those 125 missionaries taken from Camp John Hay and told they would be released. They were housed in a partially bombed out hotel in Baguio and kept there for weeks with no word as to what their fate might be. One cup of rice a day was all the food they were given. Finally, trucks arrived and the captive missionaries were delivered to Camp John Holmes.

"One of our pastors objected to our treatment," another nurse chimed in. "A Filipino house boy told us the pastor was taken to the locker. There's a locker there in the meat plant. He was taken there and hung by his thumbs. Then he was beaten. We never saw him after that."

"You are welcome," Ruby nodded. "We can use all the help we can get." No sooner had she spoken the words than a disturbance at the front gate caught the attention of the prisoners. Four Americans, an elderly couple, a younger couple, a Filipino, and Dr. Biason, carrying his injured child clung to each other as they staggered through the front gate. All were starving. Prisoners ran forward to carry them to the hospital.

Ruby quickly assigned beds and sent a corpsman to the kitchens for food. The child was taken immediately to the operating room as Dr. Nance prepared to remove a bullet from her stomach.

Dr. Biason told their story. They survived in the hills for almost a year until betrayed by another Filipino for money. Soldiers shot and killed Dr. Biason's wife and her sister. The child caught in the spray of bullets was still alive. After their capture they were held in an eight foot by three foot jail cell for eleven days with little food or water. His child had so far survived her wound but he feared for her life.

"Dr. Nance is a fine surgeon," Ruby told the worried father. "We will do everything in our power to save your child."

Of the 230 operations Ruby assisted in while in captivity, being able to tell Dr. Biason that his child would live was one of the most rewarding. Ruby suspected that one reason the guards turned a blind eye to the necessary operations was that they preferred being treated by the Americans rather than their own doctors. Medical complaints to their officers were either ignored or the man was sent into combat.

Bea was on afternoon duty, three to eleven, when a Japanese soldier stomped in yelling and pointing to his eyes. One of the doctors was on duty, and took a quick look. "Give him three drops of Ardrol in each eye," the doctor told Bea.

Bea reached for the Ardrol. Sitting next to it was another bottle of full strength Silver Nitrate. When heavily diluted Silver Nitrate can be used as an antiseptic, full strength it can burn off warts and cauterize wounds. Silver Nitrate in the eyes would be agonizingly painful. Bea studied the two bottles. She thought about those patients who came to the hospital as a result of terrible beatings. The temptation was great. She looked at the soldier. *I'll put it in your eyes and fix you*, she thought.

Then common sense took over. *I can't do that. If I injure this man then others will suffer.*

So Bea, as instructed, put the Ardrol in the soldier's eyes. The man stood up without a thank you and stomped out.

"And don't come back," Bea muttered to herself.

As the weeks passed Ruby noticed those who adjusted to Camp life were those who willingly joined the work crews. These workers stayed reasonably healthy. There was work for everyone: kitchen helpers, gardeners, wood gatherers, cleaners, teachers, the garbage detail, the list was endless. There were also slackers.

Ruby volunteered for night duty at the hospital but made sure there was always at least one patient there. The hospital sat some distance from the barracks and a call for help would never be heard. There were times when she missed the busier day duty. But the two things Ruby did not miss were the overcrowded barracks and the bedbugs.

Ruby was coming off duty at the end of a cold November night when Bea and the day shift arrived. CRASH! The operating room sounded like a troop of monkeys on a spree. CRASH! CRASH! Metal trays hit the floor yet there was no rapid chattering expected from excited monkeys. *Was it her old friend the shoe thief?* Ruby wondered. Two corpsmen volunteered to investigate. One look and they slammed the door.

"Python," one corpsman yelled. Japanese guards alerted by the commotion raced in and shoved open the operating room door to find a seven foot python stretched out from wall to wall. Sliding down from the cold mountain air it had found a warm place to settle and was searching for rats or other food. The guards let go with their rifles. Each bullet slicing into the snake's body sent a geyser of blood shooting into the air. Ten, twenty, thirty shots were fired until at last the creature lay motionless.

"What a bloody mess! Get rid of it," Ruby told the corpsmen.

"Oh, no," they replied pointing to the snake's body. "Good eating and leather for shoes."

"Did that snake get my eggs?" Bea asked.

A friend from Baguio brought a hen into camp and gave Bea three eggs. Instead of eating them Bea put the eggs under a lamp on a top shelf in the operating room. If she hatched baby chicks and cared for them she would have eggs every day.

Fortunately the python had not found the eggs. Unfortunately a few days later when the eggs hatched the three hens turned out to be roosters. Bea named them Handsome Harold, Big Red and Black Manaca.

One thing the prisoners craved almost as much as food was news from the outside. There were times when the men were taken out of the camp to work on the roads. If a guard turned his head some of the men talked with the Filipinos and brought news back to camp. No one knows how he did it but one man smuggled parts for a radio into camp. He put the parts together and hid the radio under the stairs. Had it been found the penalty was death. At listening time a lookout warned of approaching guards and the radio was dismantled and the parts scattered throughout the barracks. Most broadcasts were from the Japanese and the listeners smiled when a Japanese announcer declared that Japanese troops had just taken Missouri.

While the nurses were, in general well treated, Bea's fondness for Ching, who had run off at the first bombing, brought the nurse to a very close call with death. It was early morning and time for the shift change. Ruby and Bea were exchanging notes on a patient when they heard a whining outside the chicken wire fence.

"It's Ching!" Bea said, running toward the fence. "I know it's Ching!"

"Bea, come back," Ruby called. A guard in the distance had turned in Bea's direction to see what the shouting was about.

"Bea, don't be a fool," Ruby shouted. "Stay away from the fence."

There was a hole in one of the wires. Bea didn't see it but Ching did. The dog burst through the hole and jumped into her arms. The excited pup wiggled as she rubbed its ears. A wet tongue stretched up to lick Bea's face.

"Poor Ching," Bea said seeing the dog's ribs sticking out. "You've been on short rations, too." Bea was so involved in the happy reunion she didn't see what was about to happen. The sharp-eyed guard saw Bea by the fence. He thought she was a boy attempting to escape through that hole with the dog.

Ruby saw the danger. "Run, Bea!" she yelled.

The startled nurse looked up. The guard ran forward, lunging at Bea with his bayonet. Ching jumped up and caught the bayonet in his chest.

"Run, Bea, run!" Ruby yelled again. The other women yelled and screamed as well while Bea ran like lightening to get among all the prisoners. The guard looked at the screaming women. He could not tell one from another. He shrugged and turned his attention to getting the bayonet out of the dog. Watching from the crowd Bea wept as the soldier wiped his bayonet on Ching's fur then threw the dog aside.

As Christmas of 1942 approached the women in the barracks did their best to make it a happy time for the children. They decorated a tree with holly and made cardboard candles. The men in the shop made dolls and toy trucks. The women painted paper dolls with dresses and made stuffed animals for the toddlers. There were Christmas plays and songs. Missing, of course was the traditional Christmas dinner. Rice with a few vegetables was the twice a day meal and each day portions given out were less and less.

By summer of 1943 food rations were cut again and all of the prisoners had lost weight. Many shuffled rather than walked across the parade ground. Days were spent cleaning to prevent dysentery, spreading lime to keep down the flies, digging ditches to solve the run off problems and stretching every grain of rice to feed hungry people.

Ruby and Bea with the help of the missionary nurses scrubbed floors with Lysol, washed bedding in cold water and laid it in the sun to kill germs, sterilized and re-sterilized instruments on the wood stove to avoid infections after surgery. All the time wishing they were on the front lines caring for their own wounded men.

"If I could get to the Santo Tomas Camp in Manila," Ruby told Bea, "at least I would be closer to our troops. If the war comes to an end or we have to do anything here's my chance to help." Weeks earlier Ruby applied for transfer to Santo Tomas and urged Bea to do the same.

"I have to stay here," Bea said. "I was born near here and we have mining property near here. Right now the Japanese are bringing out the tailings from the copper and gold ore and taking it to San Fernando where their freighters are waiting. Besides, word is that they are starving in Manila. It's bad enough here but at least I know what we're facing."

It was five o'clock in the evening on September 19, 1943. Ruby was preparing for the night shift when a soldier shoved a paper in her hand. She read,

"Application for Santo Tomas approved. Departure 8:00 a.m. September 20."

Ruby had little to pack. During her nearly two years as a prisoner she had only one dress, a pair of fatigues and a tee shirt. She switched back and forth as she washed each in cold water. Her most priceless possession, however, was a mattress that she rolled up to take with her.

At eight the next morning there were hugs from Bea and the doctors. One of the cooks fixed up a small lunch box. When the priest vigorously shook hands with Ruby it was to place in her hand a half bar of soap.

Leaving good friends was difficult but Ruby had to be closer to the troops. Grateful to be able to use her nursing skills at Camps Hay and Holmes she still felt a sense of guilt that she was not where her skills were most needed, caring for American G.I.s.

Waving goodbye, Ruby accompanied by a guard and a Japanese doctor walked down a long trail to a makeshift train station. The doctor had an interpreter and asked Ruby what kind of nursing she did.

When she told him she was a surgical nurse he asked, "Why don't you do tuberculosis nursing?"

"Because I like to see people get well," Ruby replied.

Six hours later the train pulled into the depot at Manila.

The world of 6000 internees she was about to enter at Santo Tomas was a huge change from the smaller group of prisoners at Camp John Holmes. Unfortunately, as Ruby was soon to discover, it was not a change for the better.

# 9 SANTO TOMAS

The Santo Tomas Internment Camp Ruby was about to enter is described in an article by ten-year-old Joan Elizabeth Bennett, daughter of Mr. and Mrs. Roy C. Bennett, whose father was manager of the *Manila Bulletin*.

*"I was not quite eight when the war started. Mostly I remember our house being crowded with people who were bombed out of their own homes and our attempt to have a Christmas. Christmas Eve 1941 we had a little party in the house around the tree for all the children of the neighborhood. Other Christmases were not so nice. After the Japanese came into Manila they came and got Daddy and took*

153

*him away because he had written things in his newspaper about them that they didn't like. We had no chance to say goodbye to him.*

*For nearly a year and a half we never saw him. Mother, sister Helena and myself were allowed to live in a convent because mother said the enemy wanted to shadow her to see if they could find out something which would be hard on Daddy. They never got a chance.*

*Our second Christmas was made glad because we had a part in sending truckloads of gifts to our soldier friends from Bataan. The generosity of the Filipinos and neutrals was wonderful and gifts reached the prison camp safely Christmas morning, 1942.*

*In April of the next year Daddy was released and we joined him at Santo Tomas. Most of the people who had been here didn't like the place but it was heaven to Daddy and great for us because the family could be together again.*

*The next big occasion was in September 1943 when some people left the camp to be repatriated home. Daddy's name was on the list but he chose to remain here.*

*That year was not so bad for all of us children. We went to school, lived in big dormitory rooms with each person's space carefully guarded and couldn't see out of the walls surrounding the camp.*

*But we built a little nipa (palm leaf) shanty which became 'home' where a little privacy could be found and where we could grow little gardens and brighten things up. But after the soldiers cut us off from outside people in December things grew worse. Food got less and less and people began to grow thin.*

*The people got awfully hungry and what do you think they did? They collected all the recipes they could find of good things to eat and talked about them all the time, even the children and the men.*

*Our pet cats and dogs were very skinny but they began to disappear and the rats came back again.*

*Rats probably would have been in the stew pot next. The people said that cat soup was quite tasty and fried garden snail tasted like chicken.*

*People, even children, fainted because they didn't have enough to eat and everyone looked like a skeleton or else was all swollen because the food wasn't right. Then the Japanese used often to pull surprise inspections.*

*The soldiers began to get very mean, with roll calls two times a day and forcing us to bow to every soldier we saw. There was a lot of "can't do this" and plenty of "must do that." The whole camp wondered if the Americans would ever come."*

This was Ruby's future as she was on her way to the Santo Tomas Camp on September 20, 1943.

There was no talking on the ride from the train station in Manila to Santo Tomas. Standing in the back of a truck between two stone-faced guards, Ruby's first sight was eight-foot high walls and a spearhead fence covered with matting and barbed wire. With her mattress under her arm and dragging a bag with her few possessions, Ruby climbed down from the truck to see a familiar face.

"Welcome to Purgatory," Josie Nesbit grinned. "Captain Davison is ill so you get me as your greeting party." Ruby was shocked to see the once robust Second in Command a shadow of herself. Her face was gray and drawn with dark circles under her eyes. Bones jutted from thin wrists and elbows like sticks that were out of place.

"You're not exactly a beauty queen either," Josie remarked noting Ruby's shock. "Fifty-six of us were captured on Corregidor in July of 42. Thanks to Captain Davison we are all still alive. She fights for us every inch of the way. When we first arrived we were put to work cleaning latrines. Our determined Captain went to the commanding officer insisting that her nurses do the job they were trained for. She got her way. Now at least we are kept busy with nursing duties. You will be assigned to four hour day shifts and twelve hour night shifts in one of the three hospitals."

"Three?" Ruby asked.

"There is the Santa Catalina Dormitory where we lived in two rooms for six weeks when we arrived. That wasn't all bad. We needed time for rest after Corregidor and Bataan. Now the nuns occupy the first floor and the second floor is the general hospital. There is a men's ward and a women's ward. The TB hospital and a children's annex are in other buildings. We really need more space for a camp with 6000 prisoners."

Following Josie's directions Ruby hauled her gear to the nurses' quarters in the main building. One quick look around reminded her of Camp John Hay. The total space allowed each nurse was one three by six foot bamboo cot. Three hundred other women called the same building home. Only three showers and five toilets existed for the use of all. Despite exhaustion from so little food Ruby was never late reporting for duty. A quarter-mile walk from the nurses' quarters to the hospital required the women to pass through an opening in a wall between the hospital and the outside. An armed guard stood next to the opening. Severe punishment was exacted if a prisoner failed to bow to all Japanese soldiers. Twice a day thirty nurses changing duty shifts walked through the opening bowing to the guard as a group.

Ruby had an idea. She turned to the others going off duty. "Let's stop just short of the wall and go through individually. The guard will have to bow thirty times."

Keeping straight faces the nurses followed the plan. The bowing didn't last long. As soon as the guard saw a nurse coming he made a turn and went in the opposite direction. The nurses smiled when they saw him gazing over his shoulder.

There was little else to smile about in the fall of 1943 although Ruby tried to keep her spirits up and the spirits of those around her. Looking at the ever present worms and weevils in the small portions of daily rice she told the others, "I used to tell everyone to roll with the punches, so to speak. When faced with worms say 'Aha! Protein!' just what my country and I need at the moment. This I will eat for the good of my country."

A growing problem facing the nurses was an acute shortage of medical supplies causing them to find unique solutions for common problems. They made bandages from old bed linens washed and used over many times. They gathered hemp from plant leaves, pulled it into threads and wrapped the threads around pieces of wood. They sterilized the threads and used them for skin sutures. Instruments were sterilized by boiling them on a cooking stove. They made stuffed toys for the children using stuffing from already thin mattresses.

November of 1943 brought more misery. Eighty mile an hour winds with torrential rains hit the camp. A typhoon bringing nearly thirty inches of rain swept away the crudely built shanties. Made of bamboo poles and dried palm leaves the shanties were no match for the gale force winds. Electrical power failed and water had to be boiled before it was fit to drink. As Ruby and the other nurses came off duty they stopped at a depression in the road that had become a raging river. Men strung heavy rope from one side to the other. "Hold on," they shouted "and walk through the water."

Ruby's first thought was the river crossing that had nearly cost her life on the escape up the mountain. It seemed a hundred years ago. "Come on," she shouted to the others. "It's not more than waist deep." She grabbed the rope and started across. The 35 mile an hour current acted like a huge hook trying to pull her loose. She hung on to the rope so tightly she had trouble releasing her fingers when strong hands pulled her, soaking wet, to safety on the other side. For the next week crossing the water became a daily chore. The nurses soon learned to wear shorts and hold their uniforms over their heads.

The wet weather brought another kind of misery, mosquitoes. It was impossible to keep from being bitten. Ruby was near the end of a twelve-hour night shift at the children's hospital. Usually the children were cared for by civilian nurses but more than eighty cases of measles brought a workload that taxed undernourished nurses to their limit. Army nurses who were not any better off, pitched in to help. Throughout the night Ruby moved from child to child, their small bodies so weak from malnutrition that they had no strength to fight the disease. There was little she could do except bathe each fevered child with cool water.

After a long night in the children's annex, an exhausted Ruby welcomed the morning sun peeking over the top of the hospital building. She dipped another cloth into a basin twisting it to wring it out. She stopped. Sharp pains shot like fire through her fingers and hands traveling through her wrists and up her arms. She felt an intense stabbing behind her eyes and closed them tightly. Attempting to ignore the pain in her joints she stepped toward her next small patient then sank with a moan onto a bedside chair. Her legs refused to move. Hot needles pierced her ankles, knees and hips.

"Not now," she moaned. She did not need a doctor to diagnose her. She knew the signs of Dengue fever. How many cases had she nursed! She was bitten by one mosquito too many, and that one, unfortunately was a carrier of the disease. While not usually fatal Ruby discovered firsthand how terribly painful Dengue fever was. For once her will was not strong enough to force her body to move.

"Ruby, what's wrong?" Josie Nesbit arriving for the day shift found the collapsed nurse, shivering with fever, wet rag still in her hand.

For three days Ruby had her own isolation ward, a small alcove curtained off from other patients in the main hospital. She tossed and turned with a high fever, which broke on the second day, only to return with the familiar red rash on the third day. By day four, Ruby was sitting up. Her fever was down. The joint pain had lessened.

"See what good nursing can do," Josie joked.

"Nothing like it," Ruby replied with a smile. "I'll be ready for duty in the morning. The children need me."

1944 brought more misery to Santo Tomas. Authority for the camp was now totally under the control of the Japanese military. The first act of the new Commandant, Colonel Onozaki was to clear out hospitals in Manila and bring hundreds more old, sick and infirm into the camp. The first floor of the main building became a clinic and another hospital ward. The nurses' workload doubled.

Roll call was required twice a day as prisoners, including mothers with very young children stood in the scorching sun for hours being counted again and again for the counts were never the same. Much of the prisoners' time was spent standing in line, for the latrines, for a chance to wash clothing or hair at the water troughs, and for the small portions of food that grew less and less. Many waiting in the long lines fainted from malnutrition and the stench of rotten food. The newly appointed supply officer, Lieutenant Konishi, had one goal, to starve the internees to death. By August of 1944 daily rations dwindled to one ounce per person of fish and one cup of rice that resembled a thin paste, a total of less than 800 calories.

Anger coursed through the usually placid Ruby as she watched hungry children chased away from the shed where food was processed. They were waiting for scraps thrown away as unfit to eat. She cursed as well-fed enemy soldiers pushed internees aside to take over the camp garden plot and have fresh vegetables for themselves.

Ruby discovered that as food supplies grew short, one thing that calmed rising tempers was music. There were two organists, a woman and a priest who played nearly every evening. The woman played classical pieces and the priest played a jazzed up version of popular tunes. Ruby and nurses who were not on duty would sit outside and enjoy the concerts. For a brief moments hunger and hardship were forgotten. All the same she could not escape the feeling that she should be doing something else. She should have been with the troops taking care of them.

It was a difficult time for everyone not knowing what each new day would bring. News from the outside world was hard to come by. A radio hidden in the chandeliers brought some news although it was listened to infrequently and cautiously for its discovery meant death not only to the owner, but to those caught listening.

Staying occupied was important. Some prisoners were wood carvers, others were artists. Several were teachers and offered regular classes. Ruby learned to knit and did so well she took a sweater apart and used the yarn to knit two sweaters.

On September 21st a miracle happened. A roar of planes overhead brought every eye to the sky. Startled internees stopped what they were doing at the blast of the air raid siren. Japanese soldiers barked orders. "Inside! Inside!" Flying above were two groups of  bombers with sixty or more in a group. Men and women jostled for a place at the doors and windows of the main building. What a glorious sight!  One bomber came in low and dipped its wings. No rising sun on the aircraft this time. With tears in their eyes the captives saw the beautiful white star in its blue background. American planes!

Like a huge tsunami a cheer rose through the camp. The planes were bombing the bay area. The explosions echoed throughout the camp. Amid the cheers and the hugs, those who were apathetic with defeat now felt a new resolve. They would beat the enemy by surviving no matter what was done to them.

The cheers were so loud that Ruby scarcely heard a yell of FIRE! She called on her low reserve of energy to leave the windows and race down the hall. Rounding the door to the women's ward she saw Sadie, an elderly patient who had been with them for some weeks. She had dozed off and dropped a lit cigarette on a book in her lap. Tiny flames and smoke rose from the pages. Next the whole bed would be on fire. Ruby grabbed a glass of water and doused the book.

"Sadie," Ruby scolded holding out her hand for the cigarettes. "You know you can smoke only when someone is with you." Ruby held out her hand.

The old woman looking sheepish, handed over her half-empty pack.

One week later Ruby was outside hanging laundry when she again heard planes coming over. Not sure of their target she ran for the laboratory, the nearest shelter. She stopped. A shopping bag had been left in the grass. When she picked up the heavy bag and looked inside there were dozens of eggs.

That shopping bag was worth more than its weight in gold.

Swinging the bag gently to act like it was light Ruby entered the lab where Josie Nesbit was on duty.

"Any ideas as to what to do with these?" she asked.

An astonished Josie was full of ideas. "I'll put part of them in the incubator to hide them, and then each day we'll take a few over to the hospital."

Both Ruby and Josie wore oversized fatigues. They put eggs down their shirts and in their pockets. The much larger Josie could hide more eggs than Ruby. They started across the yard putting their hands up to keep the eggs from rolling out and praying they wouldn't meet a guard and have to bow.

Ruby thought of the starving children. How nourishing an egg would be. She thought of a brave woman who had been a bed patient for months yet was generous in sharing her food. So the eggs were divided up and given to the most needy. Neither Ruby nor Josie had one. Both nurses, watching the smiles on the children's faces, told each other they didn't want one.

As the daily bombings continued on shipping ports and airfields internees were pushed out of many rooms in the camp, particularly those with high windows. Under protest they were crowded into already overcrowded rooms. Japanese soldiers occupied the vacated spaces mounting machine guns in the windows and towers. By mid October, 500 more fully armed Japanese entered the camp. With them were cases of guns and ammunition. The Japanese were sure the Americans would not attack a camp filled with their countrymen.

Christmas Day of 1944 brought little to celebrate. There was so little left in the camp that even the smallest gifts for the children were impossible. The Japanese allowed a food package from the International YMCA. Each child received a small spoonful of jam and a tiny piece of chocolate. The adults, however, received a most welcome gift. Leaflets dropped overnight by American bombers were quickly snatched up. Gaunt faces broke into wide grins as they read:

*The Commander-in-Chief, the officers and the men of the American Forces of Liberation in the Pacific wish their gallant allies, the people of the Philippines, all the blessings of Christmas, and the realization of their fervent hopes for the New Year. Christmas, 1944.*

While the leaflets brought rejoicing among the Santo Tomas internees, Ruby had no way of knowing that the leaflets never reached the hands of Beatrice Chambers being held only a few miles away in Bilibid Prison. In December 1944 all captives held at Camp John Holmes were sent to the Manila Prison. Covering a whole city block, Bilibid's 20 foot high stone walls surrounded by barbed wire fence dared any captive to escape. Long hallways revealed cage-like cells, the floors infested with weevils.

"Are more nurses coming?" one captive called out to Bea. She shook her head. Later she learned that 20 Army nurses had been held there until sent to Santo Tomas. Bea, the only Army nurse at Holmes, hoped there would be more food at Bilibid. Her hopes were dashed on arrival as soon as she saw the rail thin prisoners who were obviously starving. TB, dysentery, beriberi, malaria and other diseases ran rampant throughout the prison. Few captives could raise themselves from the vermin infested floors. Bea guessed that not more than 100 out of the 1000 prisoners could undertake even the lightest of tasks. She was forced to watch as one man who refused to work was tied to her cell door and beaten. Unless the American forces arrived soon there would be no one left to rescue.

At Santo Tomas in early January 1945 a drained and fatigued Ruby finished her shift in the first floor clinic of the main building. She pushed one foot in front of the other frequently stumbling in her climb to the second floor nurses' quarters. Reaching the top step Ruby sank down to catch her breath. She felt she had climbed Mount Everest.

Never had her rickety cot looked so good even with its usual company of bedbugs. Ruby dropped down not bothering to remove her fatigues and was asleep in seconds. She slept so soundly that not even the loud roar of bombers overhead awakened her. By now American planes bombed Manila day and night. The Japanese fought back with artillery. Shells fell everyplace. Ruby partially opened her eyes at a noise louder than constant firing then quickly went back to sleep. A bomb had fallen somewhere in the quarters.

"Ruby!" a fellow nurse screamed. The exhausted Ruby slept on. Her teammate ran into the room, grabbed Ruby's leg and pulled her off the cot. She continued to drag the half-awake Ruby into a hall covered with plaster. Amid the confusion a now wide-awake Ruby found herself next to a young girl who had been badly wounded. Another nurse helped Ruby move the girl to a side room. The girl had stopped breathing,

Just as Ruby bent over to revive her, a piece of shell the size of a fist came through the window. It singed Ruby's hair, scorched her skirt and left a black and blue area on her right thigh. Had she been in any other position she would have been hit in the head. Ignoring the pain in her leg she turned her attention back to the girl. There was nothing she could do. The girl was dead.

It did not seem possible that conditions could get any worse during those first weeks of 1945 but they did. Exhausted nurses existing on six ounces of food a day continued to work. Ruby discovered that walking up a flight of steps was impossible without stopping to catch her breath every two steps. She could no longer move from bed to bed without resting between patients. She ignored the frequent blast of air raid sirens. She had no energy to move to a shelter. She had no fear of bombs. Starvation was the killer at Santo Tomas.

As a contrast to the harsh treatment given the internees, enemy propaganda regarding the "excellent" condition of their captives increased. On the way to help out at the children's annex Ruby and three other nurses were pulled aside by two soldiers and forced to sit at a table containing an empty tea set. A captain joined the group. Cups of water were placed in front of the nurses while photographs were taken. Ruby was sure the caption for the photo would say: "Japanese officials discuss the improved health of internees at Santo Tomas while having tea with nurses."

Yet, regardless of the propaganda, the roll calls, the midnight searches and one small rice ration a day, not a single nurse who could stand refused to work. Not hunger, not illness, not grief kept them from the wards. They might have been nurses with bad teeth, wrinkled skin, gray faces, eyes sunk into their sockets and swollen legs but they had a job to do. They would do that job until they dropped.

There were few medicines, no bandages, a broken autoclave, leaky rubber gloves, dull scalpels and a dwindling supply of ether but still they did the job!

However, in the opening months of 1945 the conditions at Santo Tomas like those at Bilibid Prison, were so dire that unless the Japanese surrender came soon there was little hope for survival.

# 10 LIBERATION

The race was on! It was the morning of Feb. 3rd, 1945. Just north of Manila Corporal Stanley Wisneski, a medic, and his buddy Jonas of the First Cavalry Division were catching their breath after a fifty-mile an hour race to reach the city before the 37th Division. Thousands of enemy troops stood between the First Cavalry and the city. Casualties were high. Caring for casualties for thirty-six hours without rest, Stanley, a medic, was ready for some shut-eye. In the race to reach Manila no aid stations were set up. Two truckloads of wounded followed the troops in their forward assault. It was Stanley's job, with the help of Jonas, to care for the wounded as best they could.

General MacArthur had reason to believe the Japanese would blow up Santo Tomas. The Divisions must reach the camp before this happened. The Tuliahan River was the last obstacle to stand in their way. Stanley was sitting on top of a box dropped off by a jeep. "What's in the box?" he wondered.

"Let's take a look," his buddy replied flipping open the lid with the edge of his bayonet.

"Look at that. Peaches!" He raised his bayonet to spear one. "STOP!" Stanley raced forward and knocked Jonas flat on his back.

"Sorry," Stanley apologized, "but even a medic should know ammo when he sees it." Stanley looked at the contents of the box and shook his head. The orange colored grenades did, in fact look like peaches. The shaken buddy picked himself up. He had nearly blown up himself and everyone within 100 yards.

"Now how do you suppose we'll get across that?" Jonas wondered staring at the river below.

The two watched Japanese soldiers swarming over and around the bridge. Like small busy water bugs they were darting back and forth carefully placing a number of explosives all attached to a single fuse.

"Look!" Stanley pointed to the bridge. "If that goes we'll have to swim to Manila."

"DIVE!" Stanley yelled. Both men hit the dirt as from behind them heavy rifle and machine gun fire scattered the enemy soldiers but not before one dashed forward and lit the fuse. Heavy return fire kept the Americans from advancing. All but one.

Lieutenant James Sutton was a demolitions expert. Chances were small that he could cut that fuse before the bridge blew but it was worth a try. The Lieutenant raced forward. The air was thick with bullets.

"Cover him," a Captain shouted. The men, realizing what Sutton intended, let go with a thick hail of rifle and machine gun fire forcing the Japanese to retreat. Under a heavy hail of bullets the Lieutenant slid on his belly to the end of the bridge reached out and cut the burning fuse. Cheers went up on the American side.

The Japanese soldiers, outnumbered by the American forces made a speedy retreat. Using a wing formation the Americans swarmed across the bridge. Manila and Santo Tomas lay ahead.

On that same morning Santo Tomas was a beehive of activity. Shelling throughout the city brought both excitement and apprehension. Internees watched Japanese guards carry boxes of papers from the headquarters building and set them afire near the main gate. The Americans would not get their hands on incriminating documents. Ruby saw other guards roll large barrels into the main building. They placed them under the main staircase. The barrels reeked of gasoline. *What would happen when the American troops arrived? Would they all be blown up?* Ruby wondered.

With bombs dropping all around, the nurses were worried that Santo Tomas might be blown up accidentally by the American planes before the Japanese did the deed. Either way everyone knew something was happening. A nervous excitement ran through the camp and the hospital.

Ruby was changing a dressing. "You will be just fine," she reassured her sixteen-year-old patient. The Filipino boy gave a wan smile to show he understood.

"Hey, Ruby!" She looked up to see Father Joe. Despite his rail thin frame and yellowish skin, a sure sign of jaundice, the priest made his rounds twice a day to bring to the wounded what comfort he could.

"I found some tea in the kitchen," he said. "We're going to celebrate." As she brewed the precious tea Ruby knew the gift was probably the last bit of tea the priest had. Looking at his kind face she was reminded of Camp John Holmes and the priest who had given her his last half bar of soap. They drank the tea together. Never had it tasted so good.

The heavy shelling rained north of the city for most of the day. It was hard to escape the smell of smoke from many fires. About five in the afternoon winging their way out of the smoke and haze came eight American bombers. The planes dipped low over the camp. Using their little reserve of energy the prisoners of Santo Tomas danced, waved and called out their welcome. One pilot dropped an object from his plane. His aim was right on target. A group of men ignoring the guards raced forward to find a pair of goggles with a note wrapped around.

*"Roll out the barrel. Santa Claus is coming!"*

News galloped through the camp like a friendly steed. "The Americans are coming! The Americans are coming!" Hugs were mixed with tears of joy. The artillery fire outside the camp was ignored.

One area the Japanese had not taken over was the second floor nurses' quarters. Ruby and the other nurses on duty felt the excitement that ran through the camp. A glance out the windows saw flares in the late afternoon sky that increased in intensity as darkness fell.

"What was that?" Bea called out. It was 9:00 p.m. on February 3rd. The nurses ignored the warning to stay away from the windows. A sound of heavy rumbling was just outside the gates. The rumble turned into a roar. The ground shook. More shooting, rifles, machine guns. Then CRASH! The iron gates burst open as if made of paper. A monster tank rolled into the grounds casting its powerful searchlights everywhere. Draped on the front of the tank was a glorious sight, the American flag!

G.I.s armed and ready for action walked beside the tank. There was no opposition. The Japanese guards ran for the safety of the Education Building. They locked and bolted the doors preventing the 250 internees inside from racing out of the building to greet the tanks.

At first the men and women of Santo Tomas stared in disbelief. For four years most had dreamed of this moment. In the past year many were sure freedom would never come. They watched the tall and obviously strong and healthy soldiers striding forward with big grins. "Hi folks," one young private waved.

From their second floor view Ruby and the nurses watched the camp go wild. Hugging, screaming with joy, dancing and singing "God Bless America", men, women and children cheered, laughed and cried. The children swarmed around the soldiers who reached in their pockets for any treats they could give them.

In writing of this long awaited moment ten-year-old Joan Elizabeth Bennett tells of the reaction of the children.

*"It is hard for us 500 children of Santo Tomas to realize that we are free. But we know something wonderful has happened and we are now able to shout and laugh again. We climb all over the American tanks, get hauled out from under the wheels of army trucks and tag everywhere after our good-natured soldiers who pet us and feed us candy.*

*The Americans came in and now everything is all right although sometimes we can't believe it. We hear lots of shooting around us but the kids don't pay much attention. We are more interested in all the good new things to eat. Just think, soon we will have real butter and bread!"*

"Where are the guards?" one soldier asked. The former captives pointed to the Education Building. One woman ran forward to plead with Major Gearheart, Commander of the tank unit. "Save my husband," she cried. "Our people are still in there. They won't let them go."

Two internees and a Japanese officer emerged from the building to relay the Japanese terms for releasing the hostages. After two days of negotiations the relieved hostages were released. As the enemy officers and the guards marched out in a line between booing and spitting internees, one most hated officer, Lieutenant Abiko, reached into a pouch he carried over his shoulder.

A seasoned veteran, Major Gearheart, knew what would happen next. He fired, dropping Abiko to the ground. A small grenade rolled away from hated Lieutenant's hand. Had Abiko had time to pull the pin most of those standing near would have been killed.

Despite the rejoicing at Santo Tomas the battle was not over. The fight for Manila would continue for at least a month. Food was still a problem. The little ones would have to wait for their bread and butter. The American soldiers brought all that they had into camp. It wasn't nearly enough. It was several days until trucks dodging fire in the streets of Manila brought enough food.

Given their first real meal in months Ruby and the other nurses found their shrunken stomachs could not handle the food. Most internees had the same problem. A little coffee with powdered sugar was all most could keep down for the first few days. Despite their poor physical condition, there were new wounded to be cared for. The nurses gave the best care they were capable of.

On February 5th Ruby and Bea had a joyful reunion. On that day Bilibid Prison was liberated. "I heard them coming," Bea told Ruby. "When our cells were left open and our guards ran away, I went up the stairs. I crouched behind the wall there and watched the tanks blast open the gates and destroy the guard houses. I was never so happy in my life. The

Japanese disappeared like magic. The first thing the G.I.s did was put up the American flag. Most of us stumbled out of that prison on our knees but we all saluted the flag and sang the *Star Spangled Banner* with tears in our eyes."

Bea looked in worse shape than many of the other nurses but Ruby saw the determination her eyes when she asked where she was needed. "Take your pick," Ruby offered pointing to the rows of wounded. "There is plenty of work to go around."

Ruby, who had long wished to be caring for American G.I.s got her wish. Soldiers pitched in to bring more cots to the first floor of the main building. Tables were set up in makeshift operating rooms. They carried in their buddies wounded in the fight to reach Santo Tomas. The exhausted doctors and nurses pulled on reserves of energy they did not know they had to care for the casualties. Operating rooms ran twenty-four hours. Nurses' shifts increased from four hours to six hours and sometimes longer.

Unfortunately the number of casualties continued to grow. The enemy forces operating in

Manila sent their artillery shells directly into Santo Tomas. Both the main building and a section of the annex were hit killing more than a dozen internees and injuring nearly one hundred. How much more could these nurses handle?

The answer came on February 9th. The main gates to the camp no longer existed. The barbed wire and matting were gone. A convoy of army trucks rolled into Santo Tomas. Ruby was changing the dressing on a young soldier's shattered arm. "You'll be right as rain in no time," she smiled. The return smile of relief from the boy was enough to keep her going.

"Ruby, come see!" Bea called out. What a glorious sight. Climbing down from the trucks were doctors and nurses. "One, two, three," Ruby lost count. A total of 100 Army nurses and 40 doctors from Leyte were ready to take over the care of the sick and wounded.

The work of the 58 imprisoned army nurses at Santo Tomas was finished. It was amazing that every one of them had survived although some were in better shape than others. The Chief Nurse of the new arrivals, Lieutenant Colonel Nola Forrest paid her first visit to the very ill Captain Davison. She offered her admiration and congratulations for the way in which the now frail Captain had kept her nurses together and alive. Nurse Forrest's next stop was to meet each of the POW nurses thanking them for their skills, their determination and their endurance.

On February 12th the same trucks that brought the new nurses and doctors to Santo Tomas again pulled into the courtyard. Orders echoed down the halls of the nurses' quarters. "Ten minutes to pack and into the trucks." The sickest nurses were carried on litters to ambulances. Ruby and Bea followed with all those able to walk. Neither had the strength to climb into the open trucks but were lifted up by gentle G.I.s. Every nurse grinned from ear to ear as they waved goodbye.

The line of trucks proceeded at a steady pace down Dewey Boulevard. This time the air was filled with the smell of smoke and cordite rather than the perfume of china roses and orchids. The walled gardens were broken and shattered. In place of small ponies pulling two wheeled carts were army jeeps and trucks. Shops small and large were nothing but rubble.

Arriving at the airfield the nurses boarded a C-47 for a flight to Leyte. "We're overloaded, ladies," the pilot called. "If we want to get this crate off the ground everyone move forward. Stay as far away from the tail as you can get."

The women crowded together up front, some praying as the sluggish plane picked up speed down the runway. They neared the tree line. Ruby closed her eyes. Would they stop and try again or was the ground speed too high? If that were the case they would end up playing tango with the trees. A collective sigh of relief rose as the heavy tail lifted from the tarmac. After cheering as the plane was airborne many dozed off.

It was halfway into the flight when Ruby, a light sleeper, came wide awake. What was that? The plane dropped and rose. One engine sputtered, revved up, sputtered again and died. *What now?* Ruby thought. The plane jerked crazily for a moment then steadied.

"No cause for alarm," the cheerful pilot called out. "We lost an engine but this old bird can fly on one. Might mean an unscheduled stop though. You will all get a bit extra sightseeing for no additional charge."

The nurses soon discovered what he meant when the plane landed on the Island of Mindoro. Bringing the plane to a smooth stop the pilot again turned to the nurses.

"Welcome to Mindoro. You ladies gained so much weight at Santo Tomas that we need to put you on two planes," he joked. It felt good to laugh as they climbed out and stretched their legs. Within two hours the second plane landed. Ruby was thankful there was no excitement on rest of the trip to Leyte. Trucks were waiting at the airfield to take them to the 126th General Hospital.

Ruby, Bea and the others had complete physical exams. All had worms. Seventeen of the nurses needed hospital care. Cleared to make the journey home Ruby and Bea followed a Lieutenant to their quarters.

"I always wanted to be a beach bum," Ruby joked as they were led to hospital tents set up for the POWs near the beach. For the next eight days the nurses who were cleared for home swam, laid on the beach, rested and enjoyed the best food they had tasted in four years despite the fact that they could eat only small amounts. Before returning to the States Ruby, along with the other nurses was issued a new uniform, promoted to First Lieutenant and in a special ceremony received a Presidential Citation and Bronze Star with two oak leaf clusters.

On February 20, 1945 the nurses boarded two comfortable passenger planes sent especially for them. There were two seats for each nurse. "Not exactly Army issue," Ruby remarked as she ran her hand across the top of a plush seat. "Sheer comfort." She lifted an arm rest and stretched out. "Wake me in the morning. I'll have breakfast in bed," she joked. There was no answer. Bea was sound asleep.

The soft hum of the engines, the comfortable seats and the smooth ride meant uninterrupted sleep all the way to a refueling stop in Honolulu. "Would you look at that!" Bea exclaimed glancing out the window. The surprised women stepped out of the plane to a red carpet, cheering crowds and the strains of *The Star Spangled Banner* played by an Army band. Ruby couldn't help but be reminded of the band that met her arrival in the Philippines. Would she have stepped off that boat in 1940 in search of adventure if she knew what was to come? The answer was YES!

After two pampered nights in Hawaii the nurses were winging their way to the States, arriving in San Francisco on February 24th. Another check-up at Letterman General and Ruby was on her way home for a sixty day leave.

Mardell Cottle, a good friend describes Ruby's homecoming to Spencer, West Virginia on March 8, 1945:

*"My son, Aaron, was young when he asked me, 'Mom why are people so excited because a girl is coming to town?' I said she was not a girl, she is Ruby G. Bradley, an outstanding lady, a soldier, a nurse of the highest caliber and she's our own heroine. We are all happy and excited for she was a*

*prisoner of the Japanese but no one knew what became of her for more than three years until General Douglas MacArthur and his troops found her. Aaron understood."*

Above the streets banners waving in the cold air proclaimed: "Welcome Home, Ruby." The Spencer High School Band escorted Ruby Bradley into town where an anxious crowd of young and old packed the courthouse square waiting to see and greet their own heroine. Ruby stepped from the car onto the street where relatives and friends nearly smothered her with flowers, gave her a scroll of greetings and a barrel of hugs. It was truly a day of joy.

As the summer of 1945 ended, Ruby with much of her strength regained, put away her medals. When asked to ride in Spencer's Fourth of July parade, "Sorry," Ruby said, "I have to go back to work." This time her assignment was the Station Hospital at Fort Myer, VA where she did indeed report for duty on July 4th. Although the fall of 1945 brought her promotion to Captain, Ruby discovered that POWs were not always given a warm welcome.

Beatrice Chambers describes the treatment she and Ruby and many other POW nurses received on their return to duty:

"The chief nurses were very unsympathetic They looked upon us as outcasts. They (the Army) didn't treat us well. They sent us to different stations. The chief nurses didn't know how to handle us. They put us under nurses that had less rank than we had, and they told us what to do. They said we were slow and weren't fit to take orders. They'd tease us saying things like 'that old prisoner of war doesn't know what she's talking about.' They gave us the worst duty assignments."

Bea was right. Between 1945 and 1948 Ruby played musical hospitals. Just as she settled into one, new orders sent her to another. Early one summer morning before reporting for duty in the surgical ward at Letterman General (in California) she adjusted her cap in a mirror. Looking at herself she lifted her determined chin. *Enough is enough! It is time to make a change,* she told herself. *If experience means nothing, education will.*

She sat down and dashed off her request to headquarters along with all the proper forms. The summer passed with no reply. Finally near the end of August new orders came. YES! Ruby was allowed to enroll in the Nursing Administration Program at the University of California at Los Angeles. Ruby tackled her studies with the same zeal she put into her nursing duties. In January of 1949 she received her B.S. in Nursing Education .

It was then she came full circle being appointed Head Nurse, Officers' Eye, Ear, Nose, Throat & Neurosurgery Wards at Walter Reed General Hospital, Washington, DC. Prepared to settle down at Walter Reed Ruby thought her traveling days were over.

At the end of one busy shift Ruby and one of the doctors left the ward together. "You traveled a long road from West Virginia to the other side of the world. I guess it's good to be closer to home now," the doctor said.

Ruby smiled. "Who would have thought when I was a child growing up in a small community with the values that they instilled in me then, that I would one day be involved in something that would happen so far away. When I took the oath of office, the Executive officer said, "You'll never be in a war." She shook her head and smiled again.

How wrong that Executive Officer was. As Ruby worked to rebuild her life from the effects of one war she had no way of knowing that she would soon be on the front lines in another.

U.S. Army Nurses Leaving Santo Tomas Feb. 12, 1945
Ruby Bradley in white turban.
Courtesy of: U.S. Army Medical Department
Office of Medical History

# 10 ON THE FRONT LINES

Opening new orders in September 1949 Ruby discovered Walter Reed was not to be her permanent home. "That's the Army for you," she shook her head, packed her bags and on the 25th of September arrived at a base hospital in Florida to take up her duties as Chief Nurse. The Florida beaches reminded her of her early days in the Philippines and brought a touch of longing to meet again the gentle people who were her friends there.

A first look at her small office just off the wards brought disbelief. Piles of paper covered the desk, the chairs and the tops of two Army issue ugly brown filing cabinets. It would take days to sort out this jumble of half finished schedules, supply lists, invoices and medication orders. On one corner of the desk was a half a cup of coffee so old that green mold crawled up the sides. She shook her head at the monumental task of sorting out the mess and handling essential items first.

Ruby looked up at a tap on the door. "Come," she called.

Lieutenant Archer, one of the recently arrived younger nurses took determined steps into Ruby's office. She straightened her shoulders, flipped her light brown hair behind her ears and looked Ruby in the eye. "Captain, we have a complaint," she said. "In our last duty assignment we worked four-hour day shifts and six hour night shifts. We feel that the eight hour shifts you require are too much."

Ruby stared at the girl in disbelief. "You listen to me, Lieutenant. I have watched nurses who existed on a cup of rice a day work fourteen to eighteen hour shifts. No one complained. Operating rooms ran 24 hours a day under the most primitive of conditions. No one complained. I have seen nurses so weak that they had to stop and rest between patients. No one complained. No wonder the thousands of wounded men they saved called them 'Angels in Fatigues.' It is my fervent hope that you never experience what these women did."

The Lieutenant left without a word closing the door quietly behind her.

In May of 1950 Ruby was promoted to the rank of Major. One month later on June 25, 1950 the North Korean Army crossed the dividing line between North and South Korea (the 38th parallel) and attacked South Korea. Three days later the invading army entered Seoul, the capital. The United Nations Security Council went into action. Diplomats arrived from all over the world. The debate around the U-shaped conference table was short. The Council requested U.N. members to send military forces to aid South Korea. United States troops under the direction of General MacArthur entered the conflict, which had become a deadly war.

At the outbreak of hostilities Ruby knew what she had to do. Experienced combat nurses were needed. She was an experienced combat nurse. She wasted no time in applying for a transfer and filled out all the necessary forms requesting duty in Korea.

This time there was no waiting for a reply. She received an immediate appointment as Chief Nurse of the 171st Evacuation Hospital. As anxious as she was to again head overseas, a month's training at Fort Bragg, North Carolina was required of all members of the 171st. For those new to combat the training included the levels of care the wounded received.

A wounded man was treated in the field by a medic then brought to an aid station. As quickly as possible he was stabilized then transferred by ambulance, or in many cases by helicopter, to the nearest MASH Unit, a fully equipped tent hospital ten to twenty miles behind the enemy lines. When a man was able to be moved he was sent to an Evacuation Hospital where more comprehensive care was given. The last stops were Japan and the States. This orderly progression of care did not always happen as litter bearers or field ambulances took casualties to the nearest medical help.

On September 15th General Douglas MacArthur and U.S. troops made a surprise landing at Inchon, Korea and began the push North. Five days later, Ruby along with forty-three nurses of the 171st were on their way to Korea. Each wore fatigues, combat boots and carried the helmet they were told to keep with them at all times. Two gleaming, low wing, twin engine C-47s waited for them on the runway. Each plane, known as the workhorse of the skies, held 28 passengers or eighteen litters and a medical crew of three. Fortunately there was no need for litters on this flight. The planes took off without incident reaching an altitude of 10,000 feet and cruising along at a smooth 185 miles per hour.

Ruby noticed a big difference between the nurses on board this flight and the chattering nurses she remembered on the POW flight from the Philippines to Hawaii. These nurses were quiet. They spoke mostly in whispers. Knowing that many of them would be on the front lines close to heavy fighting, not one showed the fear she was feeling. It was their small way of supporting the fighting men.

After three refueling stops they stepped off the plane in Taegu, Korea to sweltering heat. The heavy air carried an unpleasant odor. "And we brought winter gear," one nurse mumbled. Little did she know that within two months Korean winter temperatures could easily drop to 20 below zero.

The stay in Taegu was brief. The journey was just beginning. U.N. troops had regained much of the ground lost during the enemy's push south. The 171st Evacuation Hospital was headed north. Loaded quickly into mud caked trucks the nurses were jolted from side to side on hard benches. More trucks held tents, equipment, medications and surgical supplies. The smell of sweat from previous occupants was strong. The convoy made steady progress moving all the way up the line 100 miles past the 38th parallel on the way to Pyongyang where the fighting was heaviest.

As the 171st neared hostile territory near Pyongyang frequent stops were necessary. The trip stretched into weeks. Their job was to accept and treat casualties. Fighting was heavy. Many wounded came directly from aid stations. Ruby again assumed the role of triage nurse assessing the severity of head, limb, chest and abdominal injuries but never forgetting Dr. Jacob's long ago orders at Camp John Hays:

*"Everybody listen to me. We've got to stop the bleeding quickly right now! Elevate extremities. Use anything you can get to stop the bleeding! Tourniquets! Compression bandages! Hemostats! Even your fingers, if they are clean. Bring all bad cases to the operating room."* Ruby never again wanted to see so much blood.

The flow of casualties required constant setting up of tents and operating theatres sometimes as often as every five days. As wounded were treated and evacuated, tents came down and the 171st continued its journey north. "How do the MASH units do it?" one nurse asked. The MASH units were fully equipped tent hospitals with hundreds of patients. As the enemy approached they were required to tear down, evacuate patients and move within six hours.

Whatever needed doing the nearest person pitched in to help. Expecting a large number of casualties the Commanding Officer called out to Ruby, "I don't have any help. Could you come down and help?" More tents were needed for casualties. The officer and a sergeant were attempting to put up the longest tent Ruby had ever seen. "Hold those ropes," the officer directed. And Ruby did! She held the ropes with aching fingers while the officer and the sergeant tied them down. She didn't think three people could erect such a large tent but they did.

"Thank you, Mam," the Sergeant said.

"What's your unit, Sergeant?" Ruby asked noticing a familiar patch on his sleeve.

"1st Cavalry Division, Mam," the Sergeant replied.

The sergeant's words brought visions of those brave 1st Cavalry Division soldiers who burst through the gates of Santo Tomas five years earlier.

Before she could ask the Sergeant if he had been one of those rescuers he disappeared.

The fighting was fierce. Wave after wave of wounded arrived on litters. There was no place to put them all. Litter bearers had to place some on the frozen ground until death cleared a space inside for another wounded man.

The arrival at Pyongyang brought a pleasant surprise. They would not be operating out of tents. It was now November, 1950. Climbing down from the lead truck the nurses were directed to a former university building. One section was blasted away but the rest seemed to be intact.

"Set up wards and at least four operating rooms," Ruby ordered. Ruby along with the others unloaded equipment, cleaned rooms to serve as wards and prepared operating suites. Before the 171st was completely ready the casualties poured in. With the sound of fighting all around the nurses worked without stopping. While there was no central heat it was better than tents. Small portable heaters helped. The nurses worked with gloves with no fingers, now grateful for the winter uniforms they had lugged with them from the States.

The 171st Evacuation Hospital ran at full capacity. Overworked surgeons meant that nurses started blood transfusions, and sutured wounds, tasks normally performed by an M.D. Working twelve to eighteen hours at a stretch Ruby was thankful for hot food, a dedicated team of doctors and nurses and for her training as a much needed surgical nurse. Fortunately, a small air strip nearby meant that some of the most seriously wounded could be evacuated by air.

At the same time in early November the 8th Army had advanced two miles from the Manchurian border. "Major Bradley," a young captain interrupted Ruby in scrubs heading for an operating room. The captain was from a front line aid station. "We need help up the line. How many nurses can you spare?"

Ruby's first thought was to go with the captain. She knew, however, that as Chief Nurse her job was keeping the 171st together and functioning. She called the staff together.

"Up the line, means you will be in the thick of the fighting." Ruby told the nurses. "The captain is asking for volunteers." Ruby knew great pride when twelve nurses raised their hands. She was not to hear from them for nearly three weeks. Despite the overwhelming run of casualties not a day went by that Ruby didn't think of those nurses. Would they return safely? There was no way to tell.

On Thanksgiving night the North Koreans accompanied by 200,000 Chinese struck. They poured in huge waves south across the Manchurian border. They were well trained and well equipped with an unflagging determination to force the American 8th Army to retreat. Pyongyang was right in their path. The order came to evacuate.

Outside a heavy rumble of trucks rolled past the hospital. The Chinese advanced with such speed that the roads were clogged with traffic of those retreating from the onslaught. As the first convoys of wounded from the north rolled past, one truck stopped and twelve battle weary nurses jumped down . They were the volunteers.

Ruby hugged each one. "Am I glad to see you. We heard that you had all been killed. We can't wait to get out of here. We're leaving now."

Evacuating patients to waiting trucks and planes was no small task. Ruby's fingers were numb from the cold as she along with the nurses and Koreans carried one litter after another to the ambulances. Ignoring close range rifle fire Ruby made trip after trip from the hospital tents to the ambulances to the planes. Aircraft designed for forty were loaded with sixty wounded. Ruby stayed with each litter until her patient was safely aboard.

"Get aboard, Major," a medic yelled. "The enemy is right behind you."

Ruby ignored the warning and ran back to the ambulance. One more wounded man was waiting. A Corporal ran up and grabbed the end of the litter. The plane's engines roared, prepared for take-off. Bullets flew from the trees like angry wasps burying themselves on the roof of the ambulance. There was little feeling in her frozen fingers but Ruby grabbed her end of the litter. "Let's go," she said.

"Run, Major, run!" Voices from the plane shouted. They could see enemy soldiers advancing from the trees. The litter-bearers reached the open door of the plane. Strong hands reached down to grab Ruby's end of the litter and quickly pulled it aboard. More strong hands reached for Ruby and the Corporal and threw them into the plane which roared down the runway followed by a hail of bullets. Ruby picked herself up and glanced back through a side window. The ambulance she left moments earlier exploded in a tower of flame.

The wave of Chinese pushed the 8th Army well below the 38th parallel. General Walker ordered retreat back to Seoul with additional orders to destroy anything in its path that could prove useful to the Chinese. By mid 1951 the Chinese/North Korean forces had grown to more than one million soldiers. The 8th Army again moved forward in such bloody battles as "Bloody Ridge", "Heartbreak Ridge" and "The Punchbowl" with more than 60,000 American/U.N. casualties.

After their narrow escape from the Chinese forces the nurses of the 171st boarded planes for

Japan. For six months a frustrated Ruby found herself on temporary duty in Tokyo. When not caring for patients at the 361st Station Hospital she filled out the familiar forms along with request after request to 8th Army Headquarters to return to Korea.

On a blistering July day in 1951 Ruby returned to her quarters to find new orders waiting. "ABOUT TIME," she said as she slit open the brown envelope. She stared in amazement at the orders. Yes, she would be returning to Korea but this time as Chief Nurse, Medical Section, Eighth U.S. Army, which also brought a promotion in 1952 to the rank of Lt. Colonel. Not only was she responsible for herself but for the welfare of 500 other U.S. Army nurses serving in Korea. A better choice could not have been made.

1951 and 52 were years of advance and retreat by both armies. Following the Thanksgiving Day retreat the U.N. regrouped its forces to begin the push northward. Ruby found that keeping track of medical units was no easy task. Some moved every five to seven days. Ruby moved just as fast from station to station along the front lines to determine areas of most need. Hundreds of sick and wounded soldiers saw a soft-spoken nurse who cared deeply about them and would waste no time in sending the critically ill to hospitals well beyond the front lines.

There were moments, however, not spent on the front lines. Ruby never knew when battles were going to be fought. There could be two or three days of not doing anything followed by hundreds of casualties that overwhelmed the medical teams. Ruby did not write to her family of the horrors she witnessed. She did write and ask for yarn. Relatives wondered if she had anything to do. On the few "off days" to keep her fingers nimble she knitted. Nimble fingers were essential for the operating room and for emergency suturing.

One morning in Yangdonpo, (in South Korea away from the fighting) Ruby was knitting some argyle socks. A Korean friend watching her thought she needed socks. When Ruby came off duty that evening she saw her friend had completed them all.

With the arrival of 1952, close calls were frequent. It was a freezing winter night when Ruby was traveling by train picking up patients. She was about to assign berths to three wounded men when gunfire shattered a window. "On the floor," a medic shouted. Litters were lowered to the floor. Ruby dropped down and lay across a litter to protect a wounded man. Shots echoed throughout the train.

A medic got to his feet to see what was going on. He saw three men outside with hand guns. Before the medic could drop to the floor he took a bullet in his hand. More commotion. U.S. soldiers arrived in trucks. Without a fight they carted the shooters away. The passengers rose to see numerous holes in the wall of the train.

"There is nothing I have not used for transportation," Ruby laughed when a fellow nurse, Sadie Trauers, asked about the difficulty of getting from place to place.

"The past three years I've traveled by jeep, truck, airplanes and helicopter. I went by helicopter to check the hospitals. There were two trips to Japan. On return from Japan to Korea one engine went out. I did not realize the danger until a pilot next to me turned ghastly white and gave a big sigh. We landed on a sandy beach. Too bad the temperature was zero. We had time for a swim before we were picked up," Ruby joked.

"On another trip loaded with 149 medical personnel two engines caught fire. Before we took off on another trip, the pilot gave the usual instructions. He turned to me and said, "Madam, you will be the first to jump in case of emergency." I thought, *That's what you think*.

On July 27, 1953 a ceasefire agreement was reached. Twelve days later hostilities between the North and South Koreans ceased. On her way home for a sixty day leave Ruby had another surprise. Arriving at the airfield in Seoul for her flight home Ruby was speechless. Ready to greet her was an International Honor Guard and the Commanding General of the Eighth Army Maxwell Taylor who added to her many decorations, The Legion of Merit.

Sometime later Dr. Frank Haughwout offered this tribute to his friend and co-worker:

*"Concern for the welfare of her patients characterized the 37 months that Col. Bradley spent in prisoner of war camps. No matter that her weight dropped to 85 pounds, that food supplies consisted chiefly of rice, that there were virtually no drugs for patients at the camp hospitals and that the supply of surgical instruments was so meager that hemostats were pressed into a thousand and one services. She wrestled with dysentery, a balky autoclave, leaky rubber gloves, dull scalpels and a steadily dwindling supply of ether. She was finally down to just aspirin in many cases.*

*Her purpose was well served by gentleness, her quiet determination and her confidence. When she issued instructions to those who were assigned to work with her, there could be no doubt that she knew exactly what should be done and how it should be done and would expect it to be done properly."*

Ruby's story does not end here. After a brief leave at home she resumed her Chief Nurse's duties at Army hospitals in Fort McPherson, Georgia, Heidelberg, Germany (where she was promoted to full Colonel) and Fort Sam Houston, Texas until her retirement in 1963 as the most highly decorated woman in the history of the United States Army.

When asked what effect her war experiences had on her as a human being. Ruby gave this thoughtful reply:

"It made me more tolerant in a way. I don't take things seriously. When I read about these flag-burning people it makes my blood boil. These people have never seen their flag come down and another one go up. Let them see everything they hold dear go. Let them see the people they know best killed or brought into the hospital. They don't realize that freedom's not free. You've got to fight for it. People have fought for us for years. Otherwise we wouldn't be enjoying what we have today."

On 28 May 2002 Colonel Ruby Bradley (Ret.) passed away at the age of 94. As she was laid to rest at Arlington National Cemetery a firing party of seven sounded three volleys in her honor. The flag-covered coffin was escorted to the grave site by six white horses, a fitting tribute to a courageous woman who loved her country and served it well.

# APPENDIX

## Col. Ruby G. Bradley; Military Career

16 Oct 1934; Appointed to Army Nurse Corps

16 Oct 34-24 Nov 39; General duty, Walter Reed General
Hospital, Washington, DC

14 Feb 40-14 Feb 41; General duty, Station Hospital, Fort Mills,
Philippine Islands

14 Feb 41-23 Dec 41; Surgical and head nurse, Station Hospital,
Camp John Hay, Baguio, Luzon, Philippine Islands

29 Dec 41-12 Feb 45; Prisoner of War

29 Dec 41-23 Apr 43; Nurse, hospital, Camp John Hay, Baguio,
Luzon

23 Apr 43-20 Sep 43; Nurse, Civilian internment camp, Camp
Holmes, Baguio, Luzon

20 Sep 43-12 Feb 45; Nurse, Santo Tomas civilian internment
camp, Manila, Philippine Islands

4 Jul-12 Aug 45; Assistant Chief Nurse, Station Hospital, Fort
Myer, VA

12 Aug 45-28 Feb 46; Charge Nurse/Assist Chief Nurse,
McGuire General Hospital, Richmond, VA

1 Mar 46-18 Sep 46; Principal Chief Nurse, Station Hospital,
Fort Eustis

4 Aug 47-12 Sep 48; Nurse Supervisor, Medical & Surgical
Wards, Letterman General Hospital, San Francisco, CA

17 Feb 49-17 Sep 49; Head Nurse, Officers' Eye, Ear, Nose,
    Throat & Neurosurgery Wards, Walter Reed General
    Hospital, Washington, DC

25 Sep 49-26 Jul 50; Chief Nurse, Base Hospital, Army
    Command, Joint Long-Range Proving Ground, Banana
    River Naval Air Station, Cocoa, FL

17 Jul 50-13 Jan 51; Chief Nurse, 171st Evacuation Hospital

27 Jul 50-26 Aug 50; Fort Bragg, NC

27 Aug 50-21 Sep 50;Camp Hakata, Kyushu, Japan

21 Sep 50-28 Oct 50;Taegu, Korea

31 Oct 50-30 Nov 50;Pyongyang, Korea

6 Dec 50-16 Dec 50;Yongdongpo, Korea

18 Dec 50-13 Jan 51; Campo Kokura, Kyushu, Japan

13 Jan 51-19 Jun 51; Temporary duty, Assistant Chief Nurse,
    361st Station Hospital, Tokyo, Japan

18 Aug 53-21 Jun 58; Chief, Nursing Division, Medical Section,
    Headquarters, Third U.S. Army, Fort McPherson, GA

27 Jul 58-28 Apr 61; Chief Nurse, Medical Division,
    Headquarters, U.S. Army Europe, Heidelberg, Germany

14 Jun 61-31 Mar 63; Director, Nursing Activities, Brooke
    Army Medical Center, Fort Sam Houston, TX

31 Mar 63 Retired

# AWARDS and DECORATIONS

Legion of Merit with 2 Oak Leaf Clusters

Bronze Star Medal with 1 Oak Leaf Cluster

Army Commendation Medal with Oak Leaf Cluster

American Defense Service Medal with foreign service
clasp

American Campaign Medal

Asiatic-Pacific Campaign Medal with 2 bronze service
stars for participation in the Philippine Islands and
Luzon Campaigns

World War II Victory Medal

Army of Occupation Medal with Japan Clasp

National Defense Service Medal

Korean Service Medal with 1 silver star (in lieu of 5
bronze service stars) and 2 bronze service stars for
participation in the UN Offensive, Chinese
Communist Forces Intervention, UN Summer-Fall
Offensive, Second Korean Winter, Korea Summer-
Fall 1952, Third Korean Winter, and Korea Summer-
Fall 1953

United Nations Service Medal

Philippine Liberation Ribbon with 1 bronze service star

Philippine Independence Ribbon

Distinguished Unit Emblem

Philippine Presidential Unit Citation

10 Overseas Bars

# PROMOTIONS

16th October 1934: 2nd Lieutenant

18th February 1945: 1st Lieutenant

27th October 1945: Captain

19th August 1947: Captain (RA)

15th May 1950: Major

23rd July 1952: Lieutenant-colonel

4th March 1958: Colonel

# CHAPTER NOTES

## Chapter One: The Adventure Begins

Information on one room schools found in Jonathan Zimmerman. *Small Wonder: The Little Red Schoolhouse in History and Memory.* Yale University Press, 2009. An excellent source for early nurses' training is *A History of American Nurs*ing by Deborah Judd. Jones & Bartlett, 2009. The 1884 version of the Officers Oath of Office is found at http://www.history.army.mil/html/faq/oaths.html. Hospital inspection protocol witnessed by this author AFB Hospital, Tucson, AZ 9/50.

## Chapter Two: The Voyage

No record exists of the ship that took Ruby Bradley to the Philippines. It could possibly have been the USS Henderson (AP-1) that transported troops from the United States to the Philippines in 1940-41with stops in Hawaii and Guam. Additional information about troop ships can be found in *Great Liners at War* by Stephen Harding, Motorbooks Int'l, 2000. Secretary Hull's dire warning was issued at the Habana Conference, August 6, 1940. Incidents of dogs smuggled aboard ships in wartime are found in: "*Man's Loyal Friend the Dog in Time of War*" by Irene Givenson. *Red Cross Courier* 2/16/25 p.18 and

*"Merciful Dogs of War"* by Elwood Hendrick. *Red Cross Magazine,* Feb. 1917. p. 73

## Chapter Three: Paradise Found

A detailed description and images of Sternberg Hospital in Manila is found at

http://corregidor.proboards.com/index.cgi?board=forum&action.

Information about Maude Davison is found in Comeau, Genevieve. *A Concise Biography of Major Maude C. Davison,* ANC. Historical Unit. USAMEDS, 1961. Early months at Camp John Hay are described in *Oral History of Major Beatrice E. Chambers* conducted by Col. Marian Waterhouse, Army Nurse Corps. Office of Military History, *1984. pp 1-3.*8.

## Chapter Four: The Attack

A vivid eyewitness description of the Japanese attack on Pearl Harbor is found in: *Oral History of the Pearl Harbor Attack, 7 December 1941,* Lieutenant Ruth Erickson, NC, USN Naval History and Heritage Command. The announcement heard from KZRH Manila by the officers at Camp John Hay is found in The Gutenberg Project E Book: *Blood Brothers* by Eugene Jacobs, M.D. Burt Franklin & Co, 1985 Chapter One. The bombing of Camp

John Hay and Ruby's efforts to save the child are detailed in Miller-Moore, C. (n.d.) *Army Nurse Corp Oral History Program Interview: Ruby Bradley,* Center for Military History, Army Nurse Corp Archives. Ruby's description of the attack on Camp John Hay is also found in *Col. Ruby G Bradley: Most Decorated Woman in the History of the United States Army* © *1990* by Mardell DePue Cottle, R.N p.85. Instructions to stop the bleeding given to the staff are found in Gutenberg Project E book: Jacobs, Eugene, M.D. *Blood Brothers* Chapter One. Another vivid account of the bombing of Camp John Hay is found in *Forbidden Diary* by Natalie Crowder, Burt Franklin Publishers, 1980.

## Chapter Five: Escape

The retreat up the mountain is found in Bradley, Ruby: "*Prisoners of War in the Far East.*" p.2 U.S. Office of Military History and in the Bradley Oral History, pp 10-14. Additional details are found in Jacobs, *Blood Brothers* Ch.2. The mountain escape is also described in Monahan, Evelyn. *All This Hell.* Univ. Press of Kentucky, 2000. pp26-27, 32.

## Chapter Six: Surrender

The stay with the Jorgensens and decision to surrender is detailed in the *Bradley Oral History* pp12-13. The arrival

at Camp John Hay and the meeting with the Japanese
soldiers is described *in Bradley: Oral History* pp 14-15.
The incident with the ham is described in Chambers,
Beatrice. *U.S. Army Nurse Corps Oral History Program
Interview.* 1984 pp.6-7 The condition of the barracks and
daily life of the captives is detailed in Crouter, Natalie.
*Forbidden Diary.* Burt Franklin, Inc. 1980 and in Bradley:
"*Prisoners of War in the Far East,*" pp 4-5.

## Chapter Seven: Prisoner

Life as prisoners at Camp John Hay including the birth of
the baby is described in the Bradley Oral History pp 20-21,
Crouter, Chapter Two and Cottle, Mardell DePue, R.N.
*Col. Ruby G. Bradley: Most Decorated Woman in the
History of the United States Army*, Spencer Newspapers,
1980. pp 38-39 Description of the primitive camp hospital
is found in Bradley, "*Prisoners of War in the Far East,*"
p.6 and on the Appalachian History web site with
permission of Bill Gross LLC.

## Chapter Eight: A Surprise Move

The move to Camp John Holmes and the daily life of the
internees is described in the Chambers Oral History pp 13-
16 and the narrow escape with Ching who saved her life pp
55-56. The incident with Ching is also related in Monahan,

Evelyn and Neidel-Greenlee, Rosemary. *All This Hell.* University Press of Kentucky, 2000. pp 135-136.The mention of the python in the hospital is found in Crouter, *Forbidden Diary,* Chapter Three. Daily life at Camp John Holmes and the ingenuity of the Americans to make necessary items is found in *Col. Ruby G. Bradley* by Mardell DePue Cottle..p. 43

## Chapter Nine: Santo Tomas

An excellent reference and complete account of the Japanese prison camp, Santo Tomas in Manila is Hartendorp, A.V.H. *The Santo Tomas Story.* McGraw Hill, 1964.The child's account of life in Santo Tomas by Joan Elizabeth Bennett is reprinted with permission of Tom Moore, webmaster of the Santo Tomas Internment camp site. http://www.cnac.org/emilscott/santotomas01.htm

Also helpful was Nesbit, Josie. *History of the Army Nurse Corps. in the Philippine Islands, September 1940-February 1945.* Unpublished manuscript. Center for Military History , 1945.

Daily life at Santo Tomas including the incident with the eggs is found *in Bradley: Oral History* pp 28-34. Ruby's comments about the food being protein are found in Bradley: *Prisoners of War in the Far East.* The message dropped by the American planes is found in Hartendorp, *The Santo Tomas Story* p. 372

Additional information on life of the Army nurses at Santo Tomas is found Jackson, Kathi. *They Called Them Angels.* University of Nebraska Press, 2000, pp 30-32

## Chapter Ten: Liberation

A similar incident of mistaking grenades for peaches is found in T*he oral history of Pharmacist's Mate First Class Louis Ortega.* Office of Military History, Washington D.C. The taking of the bridge is found in *1st Cavalry Division, Action Report,* 27 January-30 June 1945. Filed at AGO. The message around the goggles dropped from a plane is found in Wright, Major B.C. *The 1st Cavalry Division in World War II.* Toppan Printing Company, 1947. The children's reaction to the arrival of the American tanks is described by ten year old Elizabeth Bennett. Reprinted with permission of Tom Moore, webmaster of the Santo Tomas Internment camp site.
http://www.cnac.org/emilscott/santotomas01.htm
Description of the liberation of Bilibid Prison is found in Beatrice Chambers, *Oral History.* The incident with the grenade is told in Hartendorp p. 407 Liberation and homecoming are described by Warren Scott in the *Wierton Times,* Nov 11, 2011. Ruby's homecoming to West

Virginia is described in Cottle pp 26-27. The treatment of the POW nurses is described in Chambers *Oral History* pp 52-53 Lt. Chambers reaction to liberation is mentioned in Fessler, Diane. *No Time for Fear.* Michigan State University Press, 1996. p.97

## Chapter Eleven: On the Front Lines

Chronology of the Korean War 1950-53 is found in Encyclopedia Britannica 2010

The 171st Evacuation Hospital described in Bradley: *Oral History* pp 38-40

Information on M.A.S. H. units is found in King, Booker. *"The Mobile Army Surgical Hospital (MASH): A Military and Surgical Legacy"* Journal of the National Medical Association 97 (5): pp. 650-651 The Haughwout tribute to Ruby Bradley appears in *Scope Weekly.* Feb 19, 1958.

Ruby's close calls are described in Cottle: *Col Ruby Bradley* pp 86-87 Ruby Bradley's thoughtful words about the effect the wars had on her are found in Bradley: *Oral Interview* p.37. Ruby's tour of duty in Korea is briefly mentioned in Norman, Elizabeth M. *We Band of Angels.* Simon & Schuster, 1999.

# BIBLIOGRAPHY
## Oral Histories
Miller-Moore, C. *Army Nurse Corp Oral History Program Interview: Ruby Bradley,* Center for Military History, Army Nurse Corp Archives. 1984.

*Oral History of Major Beatrice E. Chambers* conducted by Col. Marian Waterhouse, Army Nurse Corps. Office of Military History, *1984*

*Oral History of the Pearl Harbor Attack, 7 December 1941,* Lieutenant Ruth Erickson, NC, USN Naval History and Heritage Command.(n.d.)

*Oral history of Pharmacist's Mate First Class Louis Ortega.* Office of Military History, Washington D.C. *(n.d.)*

Sewell, Patricia. *Healers of World War II: Oral Histories of Medical Corps Personnel.* McFarland & Co.2001


## Periodicals and Articles
"Army Nurses Liberated from Manila Internment Camp" *New York Times,* 22 Feb. 1945

Bradley, Ruby. "Prisoners of War in the Far East," Office of Military History, Washington D.C.

Bennett, Elizabeth, "Children of Jap's Santo Tomas Camp Learn How to Shout and Laugh Again." Feb 11, 1945

Davis, Dorothy. "I Nursed at Santo Tomas."*American Journal of Nursing.* January 1944.

*1st Cavalry Division, Action Report,* 27 January-30 June 1945

Hendrick, Elwood. *"*Merciful Dogs of War*" Red Cross Magazine,* Feb. 1917

Givenson, Irene *"*Man's Loyal Friend the Dog in Time of War*" Red Cross Courier* 2/16/25

King, Booker. "The Mobile Army Surgical Hospital (MASH): A Military and Surgical Legacy" (PDF) *Journal of the National Medical Association* 97 (5)

Nesbit, Josie. *History of the Army Nurse Corps. in the Philippine Islands, Sep 1940-Feb 1945.* Unpublished manuscript. Center for Military History, 1945.

*Scope Weekly.* Feb 19, 1958

Scott, Warren. "Colonel Ruby Bradley" *Wierton Times*, Nov 11, 2011.

## Books

Barker, A. J. *Prisoners of War.* Universe Books, 1974.

Cates, T.R. *The Drainpipe Diary.* Vantage Press, 1957.

Comeau, Genevieve. *A Concise Biography of Major Maude C. Davison*, ANC. Historical Unit. USAMEDS, 1961

Cottle, Mardell, DePue. *Col. Ruby G Bradley: Most Decorated Woman in the History of the United States Army.* Spencer Newspapers, 1990

Crouter, Natalie. *Forbidden Diary*, Burt Franklin Publishers, 1980

Fessler, Diane B. *No Time for Fear.* Michigan University Press, 1996.

Harding, Stephen. *Great Liners at War.* Motorbooks Int'l, 2000

Hartendorp, A.V.H. *The Santo Tomas Story.* McGraw Hill, 1964

Jacobs, Eugene, M.D. The Gutenberg Project E Book: *Blood Brothers* Burt Franklin & Co, 1985

Jackson, Kathi. *They Called Them Angels.* University of Nebraska Press, 2000.

Jopling, Lucy W. *Warriors in White.* Watercress Press, 1990.

Judd, Deborah . A *History of American Nurs*ing. Jones & Bartlett, 2009

Keith, Billy. *Days of Anguish, Days of Hope.* Doubleday, 1972.

Kent, Eugene. *Surrender and Survival: The Experiences of American POWs in the Pacific 1941-1945.* William Morrow, 1985.

McCall, J. *Santo Tomas Internment Camp.* Woodriff Printing Co,. 1945

Monahan, Evelyn. *All This Hell.* University Press of Kentucky, 2000

Norman, Elizabeth M. *We Band of Angels.* Simon & Schuster, 1999

Romulo, Col. Carlos P. *I Saw the Fall of the Philippines*, Doubleday, 1942.

Steinberg, R. *Return to the Philippines.* Time-Life Books, 1979.

Thompson, D. Davis. *The Road Back: A Pacific POWs Liberation Story.* Texas Tech University Press, 1996.

Williams, D. *To the Angels.* Denson Press, 1985.

Weinstein, Alfred A. M.D. *Barbed-Wire Surgeon.* MacMillian, 1947

Wright, Major B.C. *The 1st Cavalry Division in World War II.* Toppan Printing Company, 1947

## Special Thanks

To Rebecca Park whose willingness to share her encyclopedic knowledge of Col. Ruby Bradley was relied upon for information not readily available.

To Aaron Cottle, M.D. who spoke to the author about his friend Ruby Bradley and made available a rare copy of his mother's book: *Col. Ruby G Bradley: Most Decorated Woman in the History of the United States Army* Spencer Newspapers, 1990. Mardell DePue Cottle, R.N. knew Ruby Bradley well and the book is a loving tribute to Col. Bradley.

## Photographs

(1) Col. Ruby G. Bradley
(2) U.S. Army Nurses Leaving Santo Tomas Feb. 12, 1945
Courtesy of: U.S. Army Medical Department
Office of Medical History

## Website:

history.amedd.army.mil/ancwebsite/Bradley/Bradley.html
Accessed 12/21/12

# ABOUT THE AUTHOR

Nancy Polette is Professor Emeritus at Lindenwood University and author of *POW: Angel on Call, The Story of a Guerrilla Nurse in the Philippines* and of *The Spy With the Wooden Leg*, winner of the International Gold Seal MOMS Award and the silver medal Moonbeam Award .

Made in the USA
Coppell, TX
08 May 2022